SAMUEL H. DRESNER /

GOD, MAN AND ATOMIC WAR

LIVING BOOKS

By the same author

THE RABBI WHO NEVER DIED

PRAYER, HUMILITY AND COMPASSION

THE JEWISH DIETARY LAWS

THREE PATHS OF GOD AND MAN

THE ZADDIK

THE JEW IN AMERICAN LIFE

GOD, MAN AND ATOMIC WAR

by SAMUEL H. DRESNER

With a Preface by ADMIRAL LEWIS L. STRAUSS

LIVING BOOKS, INC.
NEW YORK, N. Y.

LIBRARY OF CONGRESS CATALOGUE CARD #66-14026

LIVING BOOKS, INC., NEW YORK, N. Y.

Printed and Manufactured in the United States of America
by AD PRESS, LTD., New York City, N. Y. 10013

CONTENTS

PAGE

PREFACE by ADMIRAL LEWIS L. STRAUSS   7

INTRODUCTION   9

    I   Our Present Situation: *Radically Different*   19

    II   The Real Possibility of Atomic War   31

    III   The Dangers Within   57

    IV   Inadequate Solutions   77

    V   Divine Intervention   97

    VI   A Modern Parable   127

    VII   A Radical Solution to a Radical Situation   141

    VIII   Repentance   167

    IX   Biblical Faith and Modern Man   189

    X   Conclusion   217

    ACKNOWLEDGMENTS   230

PREFACE

by ADMIRAL LEWIS L. STRAUSS

Former Chairman of the Atomic Energy Commission

 THE THREAT TO MAN'S SURVIVAL which results from his misuse of the harvest of his inquiries into the nature of the physical world has inspired many books—perhaps the largest number of them only since 1945. Doubts concerning the beneficent nature of their inventions seem not to have disturbed the individual discoverers until the time of Alfred Nobel. He sought to placate his conscience by dedicating part of his profits from dynamite to the establishment of rewards for laborers in the cause of Peace—a precedent ignored in more recent years by the inventors of poison gases, napalm, and other horrors of modern warfare.

Since 1945, however, what has been described as an awareness of "having known sin" has persuaded a number of scientists and concerned laymen to review the pre-history of the atomic bomb, to describe its effects on cities and their inhabitants, and then to extrapolate its devastation into the mounting terms of a grim and minatory future. Novelists have taken up the theme and have chilled the blood of their readers with visions of not entirely imaginary holocausts.

Rabbi Dresner's book—neither science nor science fiction—and not likely to be the last essay on the subject, is *uniquely different* from those which have preceded it. For twenty years the reasoned arguments for multilaterial nuclear disarmament have accomplished nothing. The Test Ban Treaty from which so many people have drawn comfort did not stop the manufacture of nuclear weapons or even the testing of them except above ground (and, in the case of Russia, even that is not certain). It is as though the two great power centers of the world spoke different languages, neither susceptible of translation into the other. In the years when the United States could have insisted upon atomic disarmament for the world, there was either a lack of resolution to take so radical a step because the ultimate price of an ultimatum could have been war, or else because of the hope that reason would prevail in time to produce nuclear disarmament by logic rather than by force. It is now too late for the former for we no longer have the clear superiority we once possessed, and the chance of the latter seems to have grown progressively more dim as nuclear-weapon stockpiles accumulate in at least five nations.

The exhortation which this book delivers shares the frustration of the Sunday sermon that is unheard by the unchurched —which is to say, its reasoning, grounded on belief in God, forecloses it from readership in the Communist countries. Yet in the history of the written word, there have been books which have defied language barriers, censorship and even the consuming flames. Books have penetrated the most carefully sealed doors and have proliferated into millions of copies. To paraphrase the popular saying, one should never under-estimate the power of a book. And *this is a powerful book* in which the author has marshalled all the texts on the subject in support of the moral imperative that mankind must hope and work for survival.

Max Born, who won the Nobel Prize for physics in 1954, once wrote:

> There are two kinds of Hope. If one hopes for good weather or for winning a pool, then hope has no influence whatsoever on what happens, and if it rains or we draw a blank, we have to resign ourselves to these facts. But in the coexistence of people . . . *Hope is a moving force.* Only if we hope do we act, in order to bring fulfillment of the hope closer. We must never rest from fighting the immoralities and unreasonableness which today still govern the world.

And speaking for laymen, the late William Faulkner expressed it thus:

> I decline to accept the end of man. I believe that man will not merely endure; he will prevail. He is immortal, not because he alone among creatures has an inexhaustible voice, but because he has a soul, a spirit capable of compassion and sacrifice and endurance.

LEWIS L. STRAUSS

GOD, MAN AND ATOMIC WAR

INTRODUCTION

For centuries thinkers have deliberated on the mystery of our world's beginning. Today they direct their attention to its possible end. Cosmology has been superseded by eschatology.

The most pressing problem facing mankind today is not whether there is human life on the moon, but whether there will be human life on the earth.

The book before you is an effort to understand the implications of this problem.

It makes the following assertions:

> *that our present situation is radically different in nature from all previous historical situations;*
>
> *that there is a real possibility of atomic war;*
>
> *that a radical situation demands a radical solution.*

OUR PRESENT SITUATION: RADICALLY DIFFERENT

I N THE END, man destroyed the heaven and the earth. The earth had been tossing and turning, and the destructive spirit of man had been hovering over the face of the waters. And man said: Let me have power over the earth. And it was so. And man saw that the power tasted good, and so he called those that possessed power wise, and those that tried to curb power he called weak. And there was evening, and there was morning, the seventh day.

And man said: Let there be a division among all the peoples of the earth. Let there be a dividing line, or a wall, between those that are for me and those that are against me, and it was so. And there was evening, and there was morning, the sixth day.

And man said: Let us gather all of our resources into one place, and let us create instruments of power to defend ourselves. Let us make a radio to mold men's minds, and a draft to control their bodies, and flags and symbols of power to capture their souls. And it was so. And there was evening, and there was morning, the fifth day.

And man said: Let there be censorship to divide the light from the darkness. And it was so. And man made two great censorship bureaus, to control the thoughts of men, one to tell only the truth that he wanted to be heard abroad, and one to tell only the truth that he wanted to be heard at home. And it was so. And there was evening, and there was morning, the fourth day.

And man said: Let us create weapons that can kill millions and hundreds of millions from a distance, and let us make clean bombs, and let us learn sanitary germ warfare, and let

13

us make guided missiles. And it was so. And there was evening, and there was morning, the third day.

And man said: Let us make God in our image. Let us say that God thinks what we think, that God wants what we want, that God commands what we want Him to command. And man found ways to kill, with atomic power and with radiation fallout, those that were living, and those that were not yet born, and he said: This is God's will. And it was so. And there was evening, and there was morning, the second day.

And then, on the last day, a great cloud went up over all the face of the earth, and there was a great thunder over all of the face of the earth, and there was a great cry that reached up from over all of the earth, and then man, and all of his doings, were no more. And the earth rested on the last day from all of man's labors, and the universe was quiet on the last day from all of man's doings, which man in his folly had wrought. And there was nothing. There was no more evening, and there was no more morning—there was no more day.

—Jack Riemer

> A fire department which normally handles about 150 fires daily could not be expected to cope with over a million fires breaking out within a half hour (from a 20-megaton bomb striking Columbus Circle in New York City).
>
> —Tom Stonier, *Nuclear Disaster*

Silence has virtues, but mainly for the weary ear.
It is entirely becoming to the grave alone, where all has been resigned and there is no proportion.
Its charms are wasted in the wasteland:
The blunt blatt of an auto horn, vulgar and mean on 42nd Street, would, if caromed among craggy bergs in the fastness of a Greenland night, seem blown by Gabriel or Roland.
Silence has its place and seasons, even its resorts, but one of them is not the city at midday.
Hence it is peculiar when the swarming isle is still, and nothing stirs save tainted air above the cooling grid.

No use dialing "O" in the emergency: the handset is molten
and the party does not answer.

The megafire must consume itself: the fireman cannot put
out the fire in his firehouse.

The peace needs keeping, but the squad car cannot see it:
the policeman is himself arrested in his tracks.

Beware updating of a Greek god's gifts:

Prometheus had good intentions, but his brand was a miscible
blessing, like the apple that made the first two refugees.

Fire is a slave in a kettle, but a killer in the sky; it warms the
baby's bottle, but cremates the nursery. . . .

Flammable Rembrandts in the museum in the park:

Cleopatra's needle, perishable as the young camels in the
children's zoo:

Rich men enterable into the kingdom of dust:

Hotel doormen braided like commercials:

Subway riders, done in by express intent:

Newspaper kiosks, their late editions later than was thought:

The spines of bridges broken, vertebrae trailing in polluted
water:

Ships disemboweled against charcoal piers:

And, under girders and passive masonry startled into a state
of shrapnel, or burned to various shades of coke and ash,

The megadead.

And in a control room thousands of miles away, a faint green
quiver in a cathode tube, meaningful to the skilled:

And the word is passed up-channel: Bomb Delivered.

And the break for tea, followed by demolition of the country
as the first replies come down,

And negotiations continue for the end of man.

—Norman Corwin, *Overkill and Megalove*

I find myself profoundly in anguish over the fact that
no ethical discourse of any nobility or weight has been
addressed to the problem of the new weapons, of the
atomic weapons.

—Robert Oppenheimer

To all, in whatever country, who are still capable of sane thinking or human feeling:

Friends:

The populations of East and West, misled by stubborn governments in search of prestige and by corrupt official experts bent on retaining their posts, tamely acquiesce in policies which are almost certain to end in nuclear war. There are supposed to be two sides, each professing to stand for a great cause. This is a delusion. Kennedy and Krushchev, Adenauer and de Gaulle, Macmillan and Gaitskell, are pursuing a common aim, the ending of human life. You, your families, your friends and your countries are to be exterminated by the common decision of a few brutal but powerful men . . . Our ruined lifeless planet will continue for countless ages to circle aimlessly round the sun, unredeemed by the joys and loves, the occasional wisdom, and the power to create beauty, which have given value to human life. It is for seeking to prevent this that we are in prison.

—Lord Russell

(Message issued by Bertrand Russell on entering prison after he refused to "keep the peace" and call off his campaign of non-violent civil disobedience against thermonuclear war.)

BRUNER

I suddenly began to think:
Was it not possible that the Moon had gone through the
    same evolutionary process as our Earth
Before our Earth?
Was it not possible that men had come into being on the
    Moon,
Developed their own civilization,
Found the pathway of science even as we had,
But long before we Earthmen?
Perhaps those Men of Moon had found the secret of
    atomic fission long before our time,
And then had used it to blast and tear each other!
Yes, and the horrible radioactivity,

The cindered craters,
That terrible scorched devastation,
Was the record of destruction of their civilization,
A final war that had burned up the very atmosphere
And left the Moon a great cold crematorium,
Circling endlessly through an airless sky of death!

ROHEN (rising)

Really, my dear friend, I am quite relieved!
I thought your broodings came from some mysterious
    doubts of us,
Of this bright journey!
But now I know that you are quite yourself again,
The restless philosophic mind
Spinning its dialectical fairly tales!
Say, what did you think of the doctor's theory,
The—the war on the Moon?

KEPHART

It is theory

MAC

It's a helluva theory! . . .

KEPHART (shrugs)

What is the use of it,
No one will listen to him!
Talk, talk, but people do not really listen!
Talk of heaven,
Talk of doom
Talk of fall of worlds,
Of riding headless horsemen,
No one listens!
Only when the ego's touched:
    "How well you look,
You are so luminous,
So clever, wonderful,
    You, you, you!"
Do ears awaken!

—Arch Obler, *The Night of the Auk*

Howl ye; for the day of the Lord is at hand.

(Isaiah 13:6)

Every city shall be forsaken,
Not a man shall dwell therein.

(Jeremiah 4:29)

And thy life shall hang in doubt before thee;
And thou shalt fear day and night. . . .
In the morning thou shalt say, Would God it were even!
And at even thou shalt say, Would God it were morning!

(Deuteronomy 28:66,7)

1

Our Present Situation—
Radically Different

THE WORLD IN which we now live is radically different
from what it has ever been before. A new element has entered
human history, an element so monumental, so revolutionary,
so catastrophic, as to render all our thinking, all our books,
all our planning, all our hopes and fears, the very manner of
our civilization, quite out of date. This new element is atomic
war. It has catapulted us into the third epoch of the history
of mankind:

> The first epoch began with God's creation of man,
> which gave him *life*.
> The second epoch began with God's revelation to man,
> which taught him *how to live*.
> The third epoch begins now with the atom bomb,
> which teaches him *how to die*.

How to die

Man now possesses the unbelievable power to destroy himself and his world.

In the past we were horrified by the taking of a single life,
more so at the taking of groups of lives and still more at the

attempted decimation of entire nations. "Murder," "slaughter," "war"—these words have been the most dreadful in the entire human vocabulary. But the destruction of mankind itself was never a possibility, never even conceivable. Even the bloodiest battles of the past—the wars of Ghengis Khan, the Thirty Years War, the Civil War, World Wars I and II— affected only a small part of the human race; there was always "mankind." Now it is both conceivable and possible that there may be no mankind at all. For the first time enough destructive power is available—and multiplying at an incredible rate —to "overkill," that is, to kill many times over, the entire human population on our planet.

In the past when we spoke of war being destructive and of the loss of life and property that ensued, we were speaking of certain peoples and certain countries. The annihilation of the whole human race itself was never even a remote factor. Now the next war may very well be our last one.

The radically new situation we face is that it is quite probable that no one—NO ONE—will survive another war, because it will be a radically new kind of war, a nuclear war. Such a war is not only horrible, dreadful, or whatever term of approbrium we have applied to wars in the past; not only will it cost millions or billions: it may be the *end*. Man has devised the power to accomplish that. This is the inescapable reason why our situation is radically different from all previous historical situations.

A billion or so years were required for our earth and sun to be formed from primordial matter. Another billion or so years elapsed before the first primitive life forms emerged in the early oceans. Additional billions of years passed before life evolved to the point where it could survive on land. Hundreds of millions of years were required before life on land evolved to the point where a creature could emerge which was endowed with the power of conceptual thought, which could use tools, and which could control its environment. It took this creature, man, hundreds of thousands of years to reach the point where he could create a civilization. Additional thousands of years passed before he attained the power not only of controlling his destiny but of understanding the universe in which he lives. Today, in but an instant in time, he is called upon to exert that power or to forever lose it.

Earlier generations had the power merely to affect history; ours is the power to expunge it.

Complacency

That our situation is radically different from previous historical situations, and that we have entered a new epoch in human history is, surprisingly, not so easily admitted by many Americans. A state of apparent complacency seems to permeate the spirit of our country. The same little pleasures, the same little worries: television, baseball, how to get ahead—these are still the most constant concerns of Americans; the sports page, the comics, the amusement section, the stock market, local news and scandals—these are still what the American public reads first. An opinion survey "Americans View Their Mental Health" by Gurin, Veroff and Field taken several years ago reported that "problems that have a community or national or world locus are mentioned by only 13 per cent of the [U. S.] population. Within this broader category, four per cent of our respondents expressed unhappiness over problems of world tension and the possibility of war, a figure that may seem small in the era of the hydrogen bomb and the cold war."

From time to time an incredible event has the power to shake us out of our euphoria. American citizens turning themselves into human torches before the Senate or the United Nations buildings raise questions about Viet Nam in the minds of some who had not given it a thought before. The November blackout, which transformed vast cities into graveyards of darkness and fear, reminds us of the precarious nature of that technological civilization in which we have placed such implicit faith to protect us from atomic war. At such moments millions are stirred to confront the issue, only to withdraw hours or days later, as soon as the novelty of the emergency wears off, into the stupor of petty concerns which consume us.

People continue to make plans for the future much as they did in the past: buying insurance, putting money away for their children's college education, expecting to build the home they are saving for, looking forward to leisure years of quiet retirement. Their lives go on as usual, taking for granted that the great issues will somehow be solved by others.

The rapid increase in the size of American families, quite confounding modest predictions and raising havoc with housing and school facilities, implies an unawareness of the horrors to which each newly born infant may be exposed. (Some label it the unconscious natural desire to combat an impending decrease.) Philip Toynbee has suggested one way to learn whether or not the average parent is aware of the atomic threat is by asking if he has made plans how to quickly dispose of his children should nuclear burns guarantee—as they very probably can—their unbearably painful death!

Perhaps it is to be expected that the human mind would refuse to concentrate upon a fact or thought which, threatening human existence as it does, would demand a questioning of all that had been assumed, a shaking of the foundations of day-to-day living, and a rejection of the common hopes and beliefs of man. Instead, that idea is hidden from scrutiny or explained away in more conventional terms. Man has taken ages to gradually accommodate himself to the monumental revolutions that have erupted in human history.

In the past he had the time to do so: that is not the case today. To hasten the process Arthur Koestler suggested that we cease using the letters "A.D." when citing the year, substitute instead "P.H." for Post Hiroshima, and begin again with the year One (thus 1965 A.D. would be 20 P.H.), in order to daily impress upon the mind of every man that a new age had begun which breaks radically with the past. For the sad fact is that while we speak of the nuclear age, so far as the common man is concerned television has affected his life far more than the bomb, and a survey of suggestions taken for a new set of letters to supplant "A.D." would doubtless come up with "T.V."

Our children

Adults may prefer to live in a pre-atomic world, ignoring the new realities that surround them. But most children have no pre-atomic memories to reverie back into. As long as they can remember, an atomic war which might destroy the world has been a fact to contend with.

A report given at the William Alanson White Institute of Psychiatry by two doctors who had studied the reactions of

grade school children to atomic war, revealed that kinder-
garten teachers indicate a growing preoccupation of children
with pictures of destruction. Grey mushroom clouds are re-
placing the sun and sky in their drawings. There is even a
joke among ten year-olds: "What are you going to be *if* you
grow up?" The children seem to understand quite well, the
doctors tell us, that the present threat is different from all
previous ones. The following questionnaire was answered by
them:

1. Do I think there is going to be a war?

2. Do I care? Why?

3. What will happen if there is war?

4. What about fallout shelters?

The results indicated that they did think there would be war,
cared very much, described in terrifying detail what would
happen, and had little faith in fallout shelters.

To the question, "What will happen?," one child answered,
"We wouldn't be able to find our houses and our mothers."
Another: "Scientists will be pressing buttons after buttons,
sending rockets and missiles off and Russia will be doing the
same thing." Another: "The war will only last for two days
at the most because everything will be destroyed in that
amount of time." The commonest reply was: "It will be the
end of the world."

To the question, "Do you care?," one child answered: "Yes,
I care because if they start a war, many innocent people will
die because of radiation and I care because I don't want to
see all my friends choke to death. I care because little babies
have a whole life to live." A sixth grade boy said: "Yes, I
do care. I would like to live a long time but I would not like
to be just the only one alive. Even if there were ten of us, it
would be very sad."

The replies reflected a close familiarity with the reality of
nuclear war and an accompanying sense of fear. "The thoughts
of how it would feel to see everything destroyed or what it
would be like to die," wrote a girl in the seventh grade,
"makes me feel as if I want to hide and scream." Nor is there

any way of shielding a child, as soon as he is old enough to turn on TV or go to the movies or read a comic book, from the fact that we live in a world which may be destroyed.

Further, as Vivian Cadden shows in an article that appeared in *Redbook* entitled "Children and The Bomb," this grade-school awareness sheds new light on the alarming growth of teenage rebellion against accepted mores. It has its roots, largely, in attitudes of fright and despair acquired by growing up in a world where all the lessons of past generations, all the books, ideas and standards which are their heritage, appear useless, even hypocritical, since there will be no future in which to live them and no next generation to benefit from their experience. If this is the end, they argue, then what is the sense of it all?

This is the tragic new world that is beginning to inhabit the minds of our children. How can parents help them understand it and meet the fears that follow if they themselves refuse to face the problem?

About the bomb

It seems, therefore, necessary to review some facts about the bomb.

Albert Einstein had been a pacifist all of his life. But, knowing that German sicentists were working on an atomic bomb and fearing that this weapon might give Hitler unlimited powers, he urged President Roosevelt to initiate production of a thermonuclear weapon. Enormous means were provided, a gigantic organization created, and the best scientific and technical brains set to work. The result was the first explosion of an atomic bomb at the experimental station at Alamogordo in July of 1945.

Several months after the Hiroshima devastation in August of 1945, Einstein, whose formula $E=mc^2$ made possible later atomic research, published an article in the *Atlantic Monthly*, stating:

> I do not believe that civilization will be wiped out in a war fought with the atomic bomb. Perhaps two-thirds of the people of the earth might be killed, but enough

men capable of thinking, and enough books, would be left to start again, and civilization could be restored.

But in the same magazine, November 1947, Einstein reported that the bomb has been made more effective . . . unless another war is prevented it is likely to bring destruction on a scale never before held possible and even now hardly conceived, and that little of civilization would survive it.

On a television program three years later Einstein said:

The armament race between the U. S. A. and the U. S. S. R., originally supposed to be a preventive measure, assumes a hysterical character. On both sides, the means to mass destruction are perfected with feverish haste— behind the respective walls of secrecy. The H-bomb appears in the public horizon as a probably attainable goal. Its accelerated development has been solemnly proclaimed by the President.

If successful, radio-active poisoning of the atmosphere and hence annihilation of any life on earth has been brought within the range of technical possibilities. The ghost-like character of this development lies in its apparently compulsory trend. Every step appears as the unavoidable consequences of the preceding one. In the end, there beckons more and more clearly general annihilation.

In reply to a question, Einstein said he did not know what weapons would be used in a third World War, but that he could safely predict the weapons that would be used in a Fourth World War—sticks and stones!

Shortly before his death in 1955, Einstein joined with other scientists in signing an appeal which contains the following sentence: "In the event of massive use of hydrogen weapons, we must expect sudden death for some part of mankind, along with painful diseases and the final destruction of all living creatures." It was at about this time that the noted physicist was reported to have stated that, had he known what his work would lead to, he would have chosen to be a plumber rather than a Nobel-prize winning scientist. A fitting epitaph for his life and for our age!

The stage between the "small" bomb (atom) made for defense against Hitler, and the "big" bomb (hydrogen) made for defense against Russia, intensified the growing struggle among the atomic scientists themselves over whether it was morally right to make the big bomb. Terrible were the agonies of conscience with which these brilliant men fought. In the end, the Teller position in favor of developing the H-bomb as the only protection against Russia won over the objections of Oppenheimer.

Einstein's prediction was proved correct: the bomb was made. And all of civilization now hangs by a thread. One old-fashioned bomb dropped on Hiroshima killed seventy-eight thousand people. That is child's play compared to devices available today.

Dr. Harold Brown, Professor of Physics at the Institute of Nuclear Studies at the University of Chicago, stated in the *New York Times* almost ten years ago that

> A string of hydrogen bombs exploded off the Pacific Coast could kill every living thing in the United States and Canada. This radioactive dust would reach California in one day and New York in four to five days through radioactivity. Likewise a string of hydrogen bombs exploded along the line of the Iron Curtain could kill every living thing for three thousand miles in Russia.

Imagine the situation now. Scientists have admitted for some years now that there are at present enough bombs in the possession of the United States and Russia to incinerate every living creature on earth.

In the following description by Kenneth Heuer in his book, *The Next 50 Billion Years,* these figures and pronouncements come to life in an unbelievingly real fashion:

> Suppose, as do the scientists at Los Alamos, that a "nominal atomic bomb" is exploded over your city. It is two P. M. on just such a day as this. In the first great flash of light—as dazzling as 100 suns—the buildings are silhouetted against a sky of fire. Then the buildings fall.
>
> You are over half a mile from the point beneath the bomb's burst. You are exposed to a lethal dose of nuclear

radiation. You will die in about two weeks. Within a few hours, you will experience the first effect of radiation sickness—shock. In the following day or two, you will be nauseated, vomit, and have diarrhea. Fever will follow. A few days will pass when you will be free from all symptoms. However, profound changes will be taking place in your body. Then the earlier symptoms will return and will be followed by delirium, coma, and finally death. But before this stroke of good fortune, your body will become infected, you will bleed internally, your throat will swell, your hair will fall out, and your sex organs will degenerate.

During these weeks—the weeks of agony preceding your death—you will have ample time to rejoice that your family was spared by having been annihilated totally and instantly. When the explosion occurs, they are less than half a mile from the point directly under the bomb, and are struck almost simultaneously by three waves of force, each one strong enough to kill. The first (flash heat, thousands of degrees hot) and the second (invisible penetrating nuclear radiation, deadly gamma rays, and neutrons) arrive as one. A second later, the blast wave hits, crushing the city with gigantic pressure. . . .

The wave of invisible energy which produces radiation sickness—striking the human cell in the bone marrow, in the blood, and in the living tissues—arrives with the flash wave. People at 4200 feet from the explosion are killed by gamma radiation, while fatalities from neutrons occur up to half a mile. At a distance of 300 feet, city residents, even those protected by a twelve-inch wall of concrete, stand a better than 50 percent chance of being destroyed by this nuclear radiation.

These will be the effects upon you and your community if an atomic bomb, like that primitive one which killed over 78,000 people at Hiroshima, is exploded over your city. The effect that the atomic bomb will have upon posterity is still a mystery.

While the A-bombs are appalling enough, more frightful weapons, as everyone knows, have been developed. The effects of a hydrogen bomb would be far more devastating than those of an atomic bomb. If an H-bomb liberating 1000 times as much energy as the Hiroshima bomb were built, it would produce almost complete destruction of buildings in a 20-mile circle (at Hiroshima, the blast caused severe destruction in a 2-mile wide circle).

The area of total destruction of such a bomb would be about 314 square miles, so that the largest cities of the world, such as Paris (30 square miles), Moscow (110 square miles) or even New York (359 square miles), could be obliterated by the blast effects alone of a single atomic bomb.

The heat effects of the hydrogen bomb must be considered also. Fatal burns from the Hiroshima bomb were frequent over a radius of nearly one mile. But the hydrogen bomb would burn people to death in a circle having a diameter of 40 miles or more, so that the area of heat radiation would be 1256 square miles. Greater London, with its area of 693 square miles and population of 8,346,137, would be wiped out in a single flash.

In addition to the blast and heat wave, there would be nuclear radiation. However, it is likely that most of the people who would receive a deadly dose of radiation from the fusion bomb would be killed in any event by the blast or flash waves or by their effects.

Los Angeles

Another picture of what might be expected is given by Harrison Brown, Professor of Geochemistry at the California Institute of Technology, in a description of a ten-megaton bomb exploding in downtown Los Angeles. (The "Doomsday" bomb which Nikita S. Khruschev announced is one hundred megatons, and possesses the power to bomb Hiroshima with the same destructive force originally used, every day for thirteen years.)

The blast effects would exterminate virtually all but the most deeply sheltered living things within a radius of five miles. Blast casualties would be severe up to a distance of ten miles. But the phenomenon that would complete the devastation of life in the entire area would be fire. The area would be one great sea of fire, which would burn until there was nothing more to consume. A good proportion of the metropolitan area's three-and-a-half million cars and trucks would be lifted and thrown like grotesque Molotov cocktails, to spew flaming gasoline, oil, and automotive shrapnel onto and into everything in their paths.

There are relatively few facts about large fires. Several firestorms were produced by the incendiary bombing of German cities, and one such storm occurred after a fire raid on Tokyo. An atomic bomb created a firestorm at Hiroshima, but not at Nagasaki. It seems safe to speculate that in Los Angeles at least a twenty-five-mile radius and an unknown distance beyond it would be, within minutes, engulfed in a suffocating firestorm that would persist for a long time. It seems unlikely that there would be appreciable rainfall for weeks or even months; thus, the basin fire would proceed in all directions with no interference from man or nature.

It seems clear that in the event of such an attack there would be virtually no survivors of the blast and thermal effects, with the possible exception of a few persons who had made elaborate preparations for surviving the catastrophe. Their shelters would have to be very deep and provided with a built-in oxygen supply and cooling system. Unless they were, chances of making their way to relative safety would be slim.

A major problem would be trying to get through ankle-high to knee-high ash containing numerous hidden pitfalls; clambering for dozens of miles over huge, smoking piles of radioactive rubble, burned-out timber, wire and steel. If the survivor made it to the edge of the devastated area, he in all probability would have accumulated by that time a fatal dose of radiation which would shortly claim what was left of his life.

Although the Los Angeles situation is an extreme one, the vulnerability of other major metropolitan areas differs only in degree. If firestorms are indeed the rule rather than the exception, as seems likely in view of the huge quantities of flammable material that exist in all cities, we can expect the survivors of a direct hit by a thermonuclear bomb to be few in number. Civil defense preparations in our major metropolitan areas would appear, under the circumstances, to make sense only if we were willing to rebuild quarters. An alternative would be to provide for rapid mass evacuation to the countryside, where shelters need only protect against the fallout. But the time for such evacuation following warning of an impending attack by missiles would be so short that the technological problems involved in moving the people would appear to be considerably greater than those involved in providing deep underground shelters. In any event, it is evident that individual metropolitan areas are extremely vulnerable to thermonuclear attack. It is also clear that any program designed to decrease the vulnerability of these areas would be difficult to put into effect and extremely expensive. Rationally, were we to make vigorous efforts to survive a large-scale nuclear war, we would forget about our existing cities, reconcile ourselves to the loss of their inhabitants, and concentrate our efforts in other areas.

THE REAL POSSIBILITY
OF ATOMIC WAR

A Johns Hopkins University geneticist told the first national conference of scientists on survival at New York of a little-publicized threat of nuclear war—the catastrophic upsetting of a combatant nation's delicately balanced biological environment. . . . In the absence of animal fallout shelters, lethal doses of radiation would erase all wild and domestic animals and destroy the nation's meat and dairy produce supply.

An even greater disaster would be the destruction of birds, because without birds insects would multiply "catastrophically." Insects, he said, together with bacteria are the only species "fitted for survival in the nuclear age." This is so because both are enormously radiation-resistant. Six hundred roentgens can kill a human but 100,000 "may not discomfort an insect in the least."

In the event of nuclear war "the cockroach will take over the habitations of humans and compete only with other insects or bacteria."

—*Los Angeles Times,* June 17, 1962

Noah, Noah, build an ark
Deep beneath the public park.
Gather bird and gather beast
But do not gather spores of yeast,
(They don't need to burrow quite
As deeply as the adult white) . . .

Gather cottonseed for cloth
(Sheep will die but not the moth).
Dogs will die but not the flea
Tubers die but not TB
Trees will die but not the blight
Day will end but not the night.
Noah, make quite sure of fowl
Lest the cockroach form a cowl
On the crown of all the earth.
The crow is needed for rebirth.
All the Superbomb could will us
Would be virulent bacillus.

"TEMPLE ISRAEL"

Noah, when you send the dove
To the blasted world above
Sheathe the bird in scales of lead
Till the Geiger counter's read:
If it comes back from the ride
Pray for God's insecticide.

—Norman Corwin, *Overkill and Megalove*

Harry Truman explained his conviction that there will be
no atomic war. He recalled his days as a Missouri county
judge:

Some years ago there used to be a railroad underpass
where the road came in and formed two right angles. I
called the county engineer and asked him what could be
done about it and he told me, "Why, you don't need to do
anything about that. It's so damned dangerous it's safe."

They have mouths, but they speak not:
Eyes have they, but they see not:
They have ears, but they hear not:
Noses have they, but they smell not.

(Psalm 115:6-7)

America, Russia and Britain may seek to exert their
failing authority in one last effort to impose a universal
atomic disarmament, but the more realistic prospect is the
unimpeded dispersal of the means of categorical destruction. The only consolation, and it is a small consolation,
is that the very enormity of these weapons has occasioned
a revulsion from the idea of war. Even Stalinist Russia,
a state given to every nightmarish excess, drew back from
the ultimate folly. Yet for a China in a virulent xena-
phobia, for some affronted new state in a paroxysm of
outrage, to pull the nuclear lanyard at some unfixed time
in the future is always a possibility. But to do so, we must
understand, would be an act of total unreason; and there
is no certain way in which reason may impose itself on
madness. This, perhaps, is the ultimate horror. We cannot plan.

—Stillman and Pfaff, *The New Politics*

RUSSELL

> But if they've been throwing half as much as we at them,
> Or the reverse,
> Then the only loyalties left
> Are to the deepest bomb shelters
> And the lead shielding
> And the pumps
> Sucking that filthy fissioned air
> Through filters!

BRUNER (*softly*)

> What have they done
> To the beautiful Earth . . .

The Night of the Auk

> If the bomb were ever used, I would hope it would kill
> me, because the moral situation would be something
> that I could not contemplate.
>
> —Reinhold Niebuhr

> The earth mourneth and fadeth away,
> the world languisheth and fadeth away.
>
> (*Isaiah* 24.4)

> The West is swayed by a profound will to die.
>
> —Whittaker Chambers

2

The Real Possibility
of Atomic War

U NDER THE AVALANCHE of incontrovertible facts from
unquestioned scientific authorities with which we have been
deluged in books, magazines and lectures over the past two
decades and which I have drawn from in the last chapter, it
cannot be denied (1) that nuclear weapons possess the most
terrible destructive power in all history, and (2) that this
destructive power catapults man into a radically new situation,
opening before him the third epoch of human history—the
epoch of possible total annihilation.

Nevertheless, there are those who, while admitting all this,
will assure us that there is no immediate danger. The bomb
could destroy mankind, they agree, but that does not mean
it *will*. The reason it will not, they claim, is because it will
not be used. It cannot be used. And because it will not be
used, the disaster about which we are alerted is purely hypo-
thetical.

At this point one is apt to hear arguments against the use
of the bomb.

Morality

One argument, less often heard now, is that the bomb will
not be used because it is immoral. The toll of human life
that it will take is so enormous, we are told, that no decent,
Christian nation could use it. Human life is holy. The taking of a single human life may be punishable by death. How
then can anyone take hundreds of thousands or millions of
lives?

The truth is that morality is hardly a factor to be seriously
considered. Although a considerable residue of anathema and
horror for the use of nuclear weapons remains in the world
today—writes Bernard Brodie in *Strategy in the Missile Age*—
it has been considerably eroded by repeated insistence, ema-
nating mostly from the United States, that the use of nuclear
weapons must be regarded as absolutely normal, natural, and
right.

Were it not fraught with such terrifying consequences, it
would be fascinating to describe how a kind of moral ac-
commodation has rationalized one level of warfare after another until "moral" reasons are finally presented for nuclear
war and even for surprise attack. Thus, when the Germans
bombed the civilian population of Rotterdam and Coventry
at the beginning of World War II, it was considered a ghastly
violation of the rules of warfare—only to be accepted by the
allies a short time later as a necessity to be returned with still
greater force upon Hamburg, for example, where 70,000 people died under concentrated British bombing, and finally in
the atomic detonations in Hiroshima and Nagasaki.

It was America who first used the bomb. Upon helpless
women and children. Without warning. We should not forget
these facts. Indeed, we have never known quite what to do
with them. Even now, religious bodies, for example, have not
unequivocally repudiated this act. Our decision, of course,
has been defended: first, it kept Russia from participating in
the conquest of Japan and later laying unjust claim upon that
territory; secondly, thousands of soldiers' lives (ours) were
saved by ending the war months before it otherwise might
have ended.

And could there have been a third factor? Not a reason for
dropping the bomb, but for relaxing the resolve not to drop

the bomb? I am referring now to the rather obvious but little-mentioned fact that the Japanese were of the *yellow* race! For I cannot help asking myself, if the roles had been reversed, if Japan had been conquered and only Germany remained to be defeated, whether under the same circumstances, the whiteness of their skins would not have been an inhibiting factor strong enough to prevent the bomb from being dropped? That fateful beginning at Hiroshima (for which little genuine guilt has been felt), despite "reasonable" defenses of various sorts, was a blow to any future moral arguments against using the bomb, since it had already been used; or against attacking non-military objectives, since American forces had already countenanced them.

In Obler's play, *The Night of the Auk,* the first rocket sent to the moon is now returning to earth only to witness, while yet in space, the outbreak of nuclear war on earth. In a short time their ship will soon reach its destination, which is now no destination at all. Conversation ensues. The scientist-philosopher, Brunner, speaks:

> Strange, one's memory scanning under tension . . .
> I keep thinking of four students sitting in a squat-legged huddle
> On a street called Yashimito,
> Hiding the nakedness, in one small shadow,
> Of their blackened skin.
> The noonday sun blazes yellow patterns through their lidded eyes;
> High overhead the single varicolored cloud mushrooms malignant shelter.
> "We were on our way to school," one says,
> "We were talking many things,
> Important things,
> The length of crawfish in the river,
> The holiday when we would leave our books and go in fields
> To play with kites and many fancies.
> A flash, a blaze . . .
> Now we sit,
> No room for laughter in our drying blood."

RUSSELL

What does that mean?

BRUNER

On the day we bombed four students on that street called
  Yashimito,
I think you and I left the human race
And lost ourselves forever in the bloody jungle
Of the leopard and the praying mantis
Oh, we had sanctimonious phrases to offer up
For history's record:
The "Practical Considerations"
So dear to politicians eyeing history's judgment
And so, with none of that outmoded chivalry of warning
  fairly given,
We broke their back with one quick crunch,
And cheered a reddened flag of sudden victory,
But on their streets, and in their houses,
In the churches, schools, and hospitals,
In the dentist office, in the playground.
The flame of our treachery to humanity
Seared the flesh, the blood, the very genes
Of four ferocious students armed with all the terrible
  retribution
Of their abacus, textbooks, and lead pencils.
I ask you what had we done in all the intervening years,
We, high moralists, hope of Earth,
With that great treachery crouched upon our conscience?
What mass confessional has absolved us?
The new push-button transmission from Detroit?
The frosted bowels of self-defrosting
Deep, deep freezers?
A dog died on the street and we wept
The serum dripped from all their million wounds,
And their sightless, scarred faces furrowed into ground,
And we turned our heads and asked
The latest batting average of A. T. & T., and who's on
  first!

                    —*The Night of the Auk*

Balance of terror

A second argument is that the bomb will not be used because nuclear warfare has made war so horrible and the danger of "massive retaliation" so real that fear of *self*-destruction—or in Churchill's phrase, "the balance of terror"—will prevent any nation from using it. "If two opponents armed with hand grenades face each other in a six-by-nine foot cellar room, how great is the temptation to throw first?" asked the German physicist, Hans Bethe. Indeed, the discovery of the bomb is truly a boom for mankind, one might argue somewhat ghoulishly, for the fear of destruction by instantaneous retaliation (United States and Russian planes carrying H-bombs are aloft at all times) will forever deter nuclear war. No one will dare to take such a fearful chance. No country will be foolish enough to initiate such a war, when they know that they themselves will certainly be destroyed. And it is this fear, this balance of terror, which will prevent a war from ever starting and will create an eternal stalemate—not for moral reasons, but for the very practical reason of self-preservation. Thus say the proponents of this argument, the bomb need not be an evil, but a good—a very blessing in disguise. It may well be the cause of everlasting peace.

At first, there seems to be some substance to this macabre argument of mutual fear. It resembles eighteenth century reasons for the emergence of government as the best answer to human selfishness: man limits one part of his freedom in order to preserve another part of his freedom; mutual fear produces cooperation.

To say that the H-bomb is a guarantor of peace because its terrible power will in itself deter anyone from using it, calls to mind Alfred Nobel, who was convinced that his discovery of TNT was so frightful no nation would use it, war would cease, and lasting peace would reign. How innocent was he of the depravity of the human heart! War did come—war more horrible than ever before—precisely because of his discovery. Nobel died a broken man leaving a fortune to be awarded each year to the individual who would do most for the cause of peace in the world.

"The End of War" was the title of a chillingly amusing editorial which appeared in the *Christian Century* in 1909 when lighter-than-air machines were first developed:

The Wrights are attaining new wonders in France with their flying machine, and Octave Chanute, the first of recognized authorities on aerial navigation, says, "The end of war is in sight." Count Zeppelin will soon be ready to demonstrate anew the power of the solid dirigible to make long flights and regular trips between designated places, while the *Scientific American* talks about the possibility of vacuum envelopes after the Zeppelin model, a type that would do away with many of the weaknesses of a gas bag. Roy Knabenschue recently sailed about over the city of Los Angeles at a great height and threw confetti "bombs" enough to have effectually destroyed the city had they been actual high-class explosives. At the same time he effectually answered the critics who claimed ineffectiveness for bombardment by an airship of any kind because it would be impossible to drop bombs from it, thus lightening the load, and maintain a navigable position in the air.

Theoretically the Wright aerodrome should easily arise to a height of two thousand feet, sail eighty miles an hour, and remain aloft as long as the motor would run. They have actually attained a height of over three hundred feet, sailed more than a mile a minute, and remained in the air nearly two hours, and they have never tempted fate by going to the apparent limit. No gun can be trained at sharp enough angle to reach even a comparatively low altitude, and if so could not be effectually aimed at a speck in the sky going a mile a minute. There only remains the battle above the clouds, a thing too horrible to be imagined and too expensive to be provided for. Meanwhile the moral sentiment against war increases mightily and is more powerful than deadly invention.

With the invention of each instrument of war, there was always the hope that no man would dare use it. Each time that hope was smashed. As the weapons became more evil, so did the capacity within man to use them. The sword, the chariot, the phalanx, gunpowder, the crossbow, cannon, TNT, the tank, the submarine, the bomber, and now, the H-bomb. True, the bomb contains twenty million tons of TNT, but what are the limits of man's designs?

The bomb is not being used today. Not because to do so would be immoral. And not out of simple, irrational fear which guarantees an eternal stalemate. But rather out of the fear which temporary *strategy* counsels. By this I mean that it is not an emotional, total fear, but a rational, well-calculated fear, or, to put it more precisely, a "strategic" fear. It is strategy which is determining the use or disuse of the bomb. We used the bomb because we felt strategy called for it to bring a quick end to the war and save thousands of lives; contrariwise, Russia has not used it because strategy has not called for it.

The present strategy of Russia not to use the bomb would seem to be based on the following reasons:

(1) The fear of instant and massive retaliation.

(2) The vast conquests Russia has been able to achieve without an all-out nuclear war.

This latter reason deserves comment. The non-violent type of warfare that Russia has mastered through the effective means of mass persuasion, internal revolution, and cultural, economic, and social penetration—what Eisenhower called "indirect aggression"—has proved highly successful. China in the Far East and Cuba in South America are centers for Communist expansion. The Middle East and Africa have powerful Communist groups, to say nothing of democracies such as France and Italy where the Communists represent a strong minority. All over the world, Communist groups, well organized and influential, wait for evidence of some weakness in the country in which they reside—political upheaval, economic depression, social injustice—to undermine it in the name of a society which, they insist, would and could prevent such evils. As long as Russia moves ahead so steadily and successfully through indirect aggression, she has no need of entering a disastrous nuclear war.

Perhaps the best guarantee for peace, paradoxically, is a Russian victory in the cold war. (Indeed, there are some who say the free world should capitulate rather than fight. Better to lose the cold war than to engage them in a "hot" one; "better red than dead.")

If it is strategy which is preventing Russia from using the bomb and if, as I have indicated, the reasons for that strategy are fear of retaliation and past "peaceful" victories, it follows that once these two deterring factors change, strategy may likewise change. What if Russia's policy of "indirect" aggression (plus small aggressions) were to fail and many of the uncommitted nations in, let us say, the Far East and Africa began to turn away from Russia and toward the United States in economic, cultural, and military alliances, and there was a rash of uprisings of the satellite nations, supported by American arms? Or what if, ten or twenty years from now, Russia would have advanced so far beyond us in methods of nuclear destruction that she would become convinced she could launch a successful atomic attack because of an almost certain guarantee of destroying the key centers of the free world in one tremendous assault with no chance of retaliation, immediate or massive? Or what if Russia, suspicious of the West and distrusting our motives, became convinced that we were about to launch an attack upon her? Under any of these conditions, Russia might be tempted to risk atomic war!

The Russian attitude is not a fixed one. It is fraught with the most dreadful danger, and what appears calm today may turn into a tornado tomorrow. "Now it suffices to press but one button, and not only airfields and means of communication of various headquarters but whole cities will be blown sky-high, whole countries can be destroyed," Soviet Premier Nikita S. Khrushchev told the graduates of the military academy at a reception in Moscow. Nothing should put us at ease. It is strategy, changing strategy, which will determine Soviet policy.

Our concern, furthermore, must be with nations other than Russia. The small nations have, if anything, not less but more to gain in obtaining the bomb. For by doing so those differences in size and military power which defined their status are swept aside, and in one leap forward they take their seat among the nuclear powers. Never before has it been possible for a country, in a single stroke, to move out of international subservience, due to population and resources, into the class of the world's ruling powers. This is perhaps inevitable; scientists tell us that the making of the bomb is no secret. Its initial cost is great, limiting it at first to the most powerful nations, but in time—an exceedingly short time—other nations with lesser wealth and resources will achieve nuclear production.

In 1958, Britain, America, and Russia declared a halt in nuclear testing in an effort to arrive at a feasible test ban, which could then be widened to include all nations and begin to halt the headlong flight into mass incineration. But the talks were deadlocked by an apparent indication that Russia did not want such an agreement. Meanwhile the pressure to continue testing in America continued to mount in fear that Russia had been testing in secret. In addition, France was well on the way to perfecting its bomb, and other nations were not far behind. Unless a test ban was reached in 1961-62, experts declared, there was real danger that it never could be, for later it would become too involved. The test ban subsequently broke down. Russia had been preparing tests while cynically sitting at the Geneva Conferences, and the arms race rushed ahead full speed, soon to spread to other nations whose number may render any agreement impossible. The new test ban of 1963 agreed upon by Kennedy and Khrushchev once again affords hope, but also indicates how painfully slow and uncertain any such progress is, because, in large measure, of changing Russian motives.

The main obstacle to making the bomb is not *scientific*— it is no secret—but *industrial*, the tremendous cost which the present method requires. A number of countries would be able to make the bomb, but the price is prohibitive. A new process of making the bomb at a much cheaper rate may soon be available which would precipitate considerably the date when more nations will possess the bomb. A German process for manufacturing the bomb in a much simpler manner has been reported, but the facts are being considered top-secret for fear that other nations may make use of them. Not long ago Sir Charles Snow predicted that within six years he was certain twelve nations would be able to build the bomb and within twelve years some would be exploded.

As the inevitability of atomic war is accepted, the next step in the arms race will be the erection of massive underground shelters, writes Harrison Brown and John Real in *The Community of Fear.*

Eventually most human life will be underground, confronted by arsenals capable of destroying all life over the land areas. . . . Once the people are convinced that they can survive the present state of the art of killing, a broad and significant new habit pattern will have been introduced and accepted, one grotesquely different from any we have known for thousands of years—that of adjusting ourselves to the idea of living in holes. From that time onward it will be simple to adjust ourselves to living in deeper and deeper holes.

Reviewing several books, the best known of which is H. Kahn's *On Thermonuclear War,* which assume moral problems irrelevant, disarmament impossible, advocate military buildup, take war for granted, and hold that "only" forty to sixty millions of lives will be lost (apart from those who will suffer from radiation), the number and kind of shelter being a central factor, Norman Thomas observed:

I have come out of certain meetings, closed certain books and certain articles as if I had been asked to understand and enjoy a weird chess game played by governments in which millions of humans are pawns and are only a hope of double check. . . . Mr. Kahn does not discuss the suggestion of a former high official in the Pentagon that part of the furnishings of Mr. Rockefeller's shelters should be submachine guns with which the pater familias, gathering his own family in his own shelter outside the reach of blast and fire, can keep from being overrun by frantic people far from their own hiding places and desperate!

—*Saturday Review*

The theories of the military scientists, while no doubt formally correct in their neat syllogistic formulas, reveal one flaw: they do not always correspond to the human situation. That is, people do not necessarily act the way closeted theorists predict that they should act. And since the experiments are not with mice or monkeys but with men—the whole human race in fact—it may be a terrible, final flaw.

Consider the assumption of rational behaviour which our strategists make as a basis of their theory of "credibility." Credibility means that we will so make known our retaliatory capability to the enemy that, since he comprehends our capacity to destroy him even after attacked, he will be deterred from attacking initially. The theory of credibility, then, depends upon the rational behaviour of an enemy, suspicious, sensitive, divided in policy, ignorant of our intents, and open to a thousand possibilities of misunderstanding, under the total conditions of threatened nuclear war. The absurdity of assuming rationality in such circumstances becomes clearer if we consider a possible situation closer to home. What would happen, for example, if a nuclear missile were detected approaching the United States? The President, who is always within call, would be notified. What would he do? Would he at once call for a retaliatory attack upon a Russian city, knowing that it would escalate war? Would he refuse to believe that it was an attack at all? Would he be paralyzed by fear? In other words, how can we ask anyone to "rationally" decide on the end of the United States?

Limited war

Another argument is that the bomb will not be used because whatever warfare there may be will be *limited*. "Limited warfare" means that future wars will be small wars, wars so circumscribed in area and manner of weapons that nations will refrain from use of large-scale nuclear instruments.

We have ceased threatening "massive retaliation" as if there were no weapon other than those of total nuclear war. On the other hand, however, acknowledging limited wars as acceptable wars today will enlarge the possibility of nuclear war, since there is no way to contain them once they begin.

Were the United States to become involved in a limited war, in Western Europe for example, in which nuclear weapons were used, but in which it was the express wish of the participants to avoid using their all-out retaliatory forces, there would nevertheless be serious danger that the relatively small war would escalate into a large one. Ten-kiloton weapons, although considerably less destructive than those of the megaton variety, can nevertheless be used to destroy towns and cities on a massive scale. As the scale of the destruction increases, one side may deem it desirable to carry the war to the enemy's retaliatory forces and cities. Or the retaliatory forces could be brought into operation as the result of one's stepping over an arbitrary line of demarcation specified by the enemy—a city, a national boundary, or the energy of an explosion.

This is precisely the danger we face in Vietnam. It is a danger which looms all the larger when we recall that, in the face of all we know of the nuclear horror, a presidential candidate, Barry Goldwater, could express the ultimate in casual irresponsibility by advocating seriously "defoliating" the Vietnam jungle with atomic bombs and suggesting jokingly that we "lob one into the men's room of the Kremlin."

There is only one difficulty with the theory of limited warfare: there is absolutely nothing to guarantee that it will *remain* limited. The term "limited warfare" is ultimately self-contradictory. No one can guarantee that the arbitrary conditions and prearrangements of any restricted combat will not, in the course of battle, burst into all-out conflict. Warfare by its very nature cannot be limited or restricted. If defeat threatens or opportunity appears, what was limited will become unlimited. Limited warfare when applied to the atomic age is like standing around a furnace into which sticks of dynamite wrapped in special asbestos covers have been thrown, and relying upon this protection.

Unpredictability

Lastly, what is to prevent nuclear war from beginning as a result of such unpredictable causes as mechanical accident or human error?

Russia and the United States are at a trigger-edge readiness to retaliate instantly and massively at the first sign of attack. Victory, or even survival, may depend on the number of seconds that pass between recognition of attack and response. Our soldiers, scientists, and pilots, as well as theirs, are being trained to split-second efficiency in order to get planes and missiles into the air in the shortest possible time after the first warning. Each second is important; every possible means is examined to reduce the time element. The United States and Russia both have planes carrying H-bombs in the air at all times to facilitate retaliation. The men involved in these undertakings are under a constant and terrible strain. The tension is almost unbearable. It is perfectly plausible, therefore, that some one of the thousands of men involved could commit an error either in assuming that the bomb is coming or in setting off the bomb. Once this happens there is no going back. The war is on. And what of accidents due to faulty mechanisms, be they ever so thoroughly checked? It is true that the problem has been realized and risks reduced by all kinds of precautions; but, it is, alas, likewise true that no one can conceive of every possibility, and the human body and humanly-fashioned machines are fallible. We cannot afford the luxury of fallibility in this case.

> Military Chiefs have human bellies,
> Human nerve-ends, human backsides,
> And that push-button war could well have started
> From a belly-ache, a nervous tremor,
> Too much Vodka, or a short-circuit in a San Francisco
> standby—   *—The Night of the Auk*

Several years ago our massive radar screens in the north picked up a flying object approaching the United States. It was unidentified. Jet bombers containing the bomb—which are always in the air hovering near the Russian border to prevent Russians from believing a surprise attack would not likewise destroy them even if our country lay in ruins—were immediately signaled to move toward the Soviet capital. Fortunately, there was time to recall them when it became clear that the "unidentified objects" were—a migratory group of birds!

More recently the highly complicated system of alarms—six in all—which was devised to prevent such accidents was itself almost fooled. The radar screen again recorded a strange object approaching our country. This time Alarm number One flashed ("watch closely"), then number Two ("Be ready to move in seconds"), Three ("Something definitely coming, contact Washington"), Four ("You are apparently under attack") Five ("It is 99.97 percent certain you are under ICBM attack"). This seemed to be it. A split-second decision had to be made whether or not to push Number Six and send our rockets winging into space, for if a Russian missile was indeed on its way, it would be too late to delay any later. Only at that last breathless moment did the spine-tingling truth become known—the moon was rising and had been tracked on the radar screen!

These are but two cases which the military has made known to the public. How many such hair-trigger misses have gone unreported? How many in Russia? And do we not contribute each to the other's rate of accident?

It was estimated that two thousand of our bombers—some in training, others carrying the bomb—make almost 100,000 missions a year toward Russia and back, just to guarantee that our planes are in the air at all times. We have been at this for about ten years, approximating one million such missions. Now assuming only the smallest percentage of accidents to be allowed for human fallability—a pilot gone mad under unbearable pressure, instructions misinterpreted, etc.—multiply this by the Russian pilots and all those military people directly involved, and we must shudder to draw the almost inevitable conclusion. For any accident must trigger the instantaneous defense retaliation of the other power.

> Over the long run it does not matter how small the probability of an accident is per unit time—said the distinguished scientist, H. Lustig—it is mathematically demonstrable that as time goes on, this probability approaches certainty.

H. Burdick, the author (along with H. Wheeler) of *Failsafe* was asked in an interview: "Based on your knowledge of the failsafe system, what are the chances that the kind of accident you describe in your book could actually happen?"

> I believe it to be inevitable under the present circumstances—he replied—that is why we wrote this book. I don't know of a scientist who has a direct knowledge of 'failsafe' who isn't worried.

The assassination of President John F. Kennedy, Norman Cousins points out, may serve as a paradigm to our dilemma.

Our immediate reaction to the tragedy was one of unbelief. Somehow the human imagination had not projected such a possibility; it was simply outside its range. Then a disturbed mind, brooding in a hate-filled atmosphere, fired a gun, and the human mind was staggered. When people said they could not believe it had happened, they were in fact saying that it was incredible to acknowledge that a single senseless person had sent a nation into shock.

But that is exactly our situation in regard to nuclear war. One person can set off that blast which will destroy not just a single president, but the entire world. We have arrived at the point where the "assassination" of mankind is just such a probability.

For, consider, is it not true that both the United States and Russia maintain submarines near the coasts of the other's shores with nuclear-topped missiles that can reach most of the major cities, that the United States operates hundreds of planes on a round-the-clock basis near the border of Russia, and that these planes are equipped with nuclear bombs? Despite the fact that the selection of the submarine and plane commanders is carried out with exceptional care and constant security and that vigilance and other precautions are maintained, the glaring fact remains that the terrible power to detonate a nuclear bomb is placed in the hands of hundreds of men. And we know enough of the human species to be absolutely sure of one thing: heir to folly and foible, he is never completely predictable. No ironclad guarantee will ever be given us from any psychiatrist that one of these men will not disobey orders, for any one of a number of reasons. Who knows what suspicion, what hatred, what deep-seated feeling lurks in his soul. "The heart of man," says the prophet, "is deceitful above all things." Indeed, such action could well be motivated by the noblest of motives: patriotism, the serving of his country, ridding the world of the Communist menace.

Cousins mentions that in the Algerian war a French pilot, distraught at what he considered a bankrupt policy of his government, bombed—on his own initiative and against all orders—an Algerian village. True, that was only one pilot gone berserk out of many thousands, but this is precisely the point!

When will we learn that what distinguishes our dilemma from all previous dilemmas, what makes our situation truly *sui generis*, is that one single human being can assassinate mankind?

The defenses which have been erected against irrational action in handling the mightiest power on earth are enormously elaborate. So were the defenses against the attack upon the President. Most of the precautions we have been, and are, taking are against accidental warfare, but what about the danger of "arbitrary decision?" What precaution is there against the most unpredictable thing in all the world, man?

Every society—writes psychiatrist Dr. Jerome Frank—contains a small portion of unstable or evil persons who delight in destruction and who cannot be detected by ordinary screening devices. Unless the spread of weapons is halted, it is a statistical certainty that eventually someone like this will get the chance to fire a weapon that can kill millions and so precipitate a worldwide catastrophe.

Furthermore, our attempt to make credible to the enemy the fact that, even if they succeed in destroying our means of governing ourselves by obliterating Washington and New York, they can never destroy the certainty of retaliation, is evidence of our madness. For what we are affirming is that, no matter how many are killed, there will always be those in charge of planes, submarines, missiles, etc., who can detonate the charge. True, only a few can give the signal for war, but many—too many—can explode a bomb. And we rely on the credibility of this belief—the certainty of retaliation, no matter how great the destruction—to prevent a nuclear strike.

We are faced during the course of the next twenty-five years with the prospect of seeing one nation after another achieve the means of manufacturing nuclear explosives, and of delivering them with planes, missiles and submarines. With the addition of each new nation to the list, the problem of achieving control of any sort will increase enormously. As missiles become more dependable agents for delivery, increased emphasis will be placed upon the use of nuclear explosives for defensive purposes. Eventually most nations will be heavily armed with these weapons.

Within this anarchic framework there will be "little wars in which tactical nuclear weapons will be used. We are asked to believe that human beings will handle themselves intelligently and cooly in these wars and that everyone's ability to retaliate with massive destruction will result in stabilization. No nation, it is argued, will employ H-bombs strategically for fear of being destroyed herself.

The degree of wishful thinking involved in this view is, I believe, fantastic. In a rapidly changing world, such a situation would be about as stable as a billiard ball balanced on a pinhead. To persons who doubt this, I can only say that a Tunisian village was bombed the other day as the result of an order given by an officer who acted rashly and without the knowledge of the government of France. This was not the first time a French officer has taken a rash action on his own, and it may not be the last.

Imagine, if you will, a world in which nuclear weapons of all sizes have become commonplace and widespread. Couple this with the ever-present possibility of rash military action such as we have witnessed in Tunisia. Add to this the prospect that rash actions can be precipitated in virtually every region of the globe. Mix with this the consideration that individual human beings are more likely to act in a crisis on the basis of considered judgment. Add to this the extent to which ignorance permeates human society. Add, for what it is worth, our knowledge from past history concerning the frequency of occurrence of wars. Now examine all of these factors and ask yourselves for how long a time you honestly believe violence on a large scale can be avoided. Our opinions will, of course, vary. But I believe that most of us who are able to divorce ourselves from our tendency to indulge in wishful thinking would agree that the time that stands between us and large scale disaster some place in the world is agonizingly short.

—H. Brown, *The Reporter*

It must seem clear, therefore, that there is no sure prevention of atomic war. We live under daily threat of total annihilation.

Madness

When I look out upon this world of music and poetry and starlit skies and flowers and love and friendship and glory and grandeur, and contemplate that it may all go up in a wisp of smoke—that man has transformed God's vision of earth into a nightmare—then the words of the holy Zaddik, Rabbi Nahman of Bratslav, spoken a century and a half ago, ring in my ears.

Long ago in a land beyond the seas, terrible prophecy was revealed to the king one night through the magic of the stars:

"The crops of the next harvest will be cursed, and whoever eats of them will go mad!"

At once the king gathered together from near and far his wisest advisors to take counsel as to how they might meet the approaching calamity. Many proposals were made by the nobles but all were rejected. For the alternatives were equally and terribly clear: if they ate the food they would go mad; if they refused to eat they would die of starvation. Madness or death; which should the choice be?

At last, in despair, they turned to the king, and he spoke:

> Since there will be no food other than that which is cursed, we have no course but to eat and remain alive.
>
> But—he added, addressing his most faithful counselor— I have still enough provisions to save one man. I shall put them in your house so that you may escape the common fate. This will be your duty: when we have all lost our senses, you will ride through the kingdom, and in all the streets of the cities, in the shops, the squares, the markets, in the fields before the cottages, you will cry out:
>
> "My brothers, my brothers. Remember that you are mad!"

The mystery of Rabbi Nahman's parable, handed down to the initiate for one hundred and fifty years, has waited until

our generation to be understood by all in the terrible fullness
of its meaning.

We today are confronted by apparently impossible alternatives:

(1) to live *without* the bomb, that is, as if we had never
known it, thanks to some wondrous time-machine which
might sweep us back through the centuries—even one
century—and keep us there forever, expunging from our
minds and manuals every last trace of atomic know-how.
But, alas, we have no time-machine!

(2) to live *with* the bomb, that is, as if we possessed some
secret elixir which, reduced to fine powder and scattered
through the atmosphere above each country, would won-
drously render nuclear energy impotent when used for
destructive purposes, such as war, and potent when used
for peaceful purposes, such as curing disease, feeding the
hungry, and rebuilding our cities. But, alas, we have no
elixir!

Is there a choice?

We have no option but to live with the bomb. But at least
let us not delude ourselves into believing that the world in
which we live is the very same world—quite unchanged in its
fears and hopes and realities—which existed before the bomb.

Let us confess that a creature possessing mind and soul, who
can reason and pray, philosophize and prophesy, is the bearer
of His word, the witness to His truth, the living symbol of His
reality, and who possesses the power to fashion a paradise—
but instead turns his genius to the manufacture of what may
very well produce a human inferno—must be mad.

We have eaten poisoned food. Our earth has become a
vast lunatic asylum. But we persist in the illusion that we are
sane. We buy and sell, tear down and build, marry and have
children, campaign and govern, even teach and preach—as if
nothing had changed.

Are we sane?

Is it sane to order our world in such a way that it might
explode in our hands at any moment like some maniac's time-

bomb, and nonchalantly go about our accustomed ways, stuffing our ears with cotton so as not to hear the ticking?

If the attempted suicide of one man is diagnosed as a sign of mental illness, what shall we say of the planned self-immolation of all men? Is the creature sane or mad who swears from the roof top that he wishes nothing so dearly as peace and then spends a hundred and sixty billion dollars a year employing the wisest minds, the greatest engines, and a goodly portion of the entire productive power of the earth planning death weapons, one more hideous than the other, which contain sufficient power to destroy every human being one hundred times over?

Do we hear the appointed one's desperate cries, almost muffled by the thunder of the street, reminding us of our madness?

And if we hear the sound, do we hearken to the words?

And if we hearken, what can we do?

Can those who are mad regain their sanity?

THE DANGERS WITHIN

At first God made a paradise and drove man from it. Now man has made a paradise of his own from which he has driven God.

—A. Heschel

Did you know there are six hundred thousand patients in mental hospitals in the United States today, and that they are increasing at the rate of 200,000 a year? Did you know that fourteen million persons now living in this country will suffer a serious nervous breakdown sometime in their lives? Did you know that fifty percent of all military draftees who were rejected, were rejected for this reason, and that thirty-eight percent of all service men who were discharged, were discharged for this cause? Did you know that there are one hundred thousand attempted suicides in this country every year, and four million citizens who are disabled by alcoholism?

That means—says the doctor who gave us these figures —that the strain of life in America today is so great that large numbers of people cannot meet it without either going to pieces or seeking to destroy themselves totally or partially.

—Author Unknown

And it shall be, when the Lord thy God shall bring thee into the land which He swore unto thy fathers, to Abraham, to Isaac, and to Jacob, to give thee—great and goodly cities, which thou didst not build, and houses full of all good things, which thou didst not fill, and cisterns hewn out, which thou didst not hew, vineyards and olive-trees, which thou didst not plant, and thou shalt eat and be satisfied—then beware lest thou forget the Lord, who brought thee out of the land of Egypt, out of the house of bondage.

(*Deut. 6:10-12*)

The dying world had no answer at all to the crisis of the 20th century, and, when it was mentioned, and every moral voice in the Western world was shrilling crisis, it cocked an ear of complacent deafness and smiled a smile of blank senility—throughout history, the smile of those for whom the executioner waits.

—Whittaker Chambers

But Jeshurun waxed fat, and kicked—
Thou didst wax fat, thou didst grow thick, thou didst
    become gross—
And he forsook God who made him.

(*Deut.* 32.15)

Someone has to reinspect our system and that soon. We can't expect to raise our children to be good and honorable men when the city, the state, the government, the corporations all offer higher rewards for chicanery and deceit than for probity and truth.

—John Steinbeck

There is little sense of shock anymore.

—Bishop J. Pike

3

The Dangers Within

THE DANGERS without are sufficiently overwhelming, but what of the dangers within? There is no question but that Russia represents a nation committed to a purpose in which it believes wholeheartedly. The imminent collapse of Russian Communism which American writers confidently predicted has not taken place. Instead we are being shown that it is possible—at least for a time—to establish an imperialistic society, lacking the elementary guarantees of Western freedom, personal and political, but devoted to a future hope of world domination which successfully mobilizes the thought and the lives of a complex association of peoples. The belief that the capitalist society of the West will ultimately be supplanted by the Communist society of the East is that central dogma of Russia which undergirds all their planning, guarantees all their sacrifice, and justifies itself on an increasing level.

Mr. Khrushchev—wrote Walter Lippmann after returning from a personal meeting with the Soviet ruler—is a true believer that Communism is destined to supplant

Capitalism, as Capitalism supplanted Feudalism. For him this is an absolute dogma, and he will tell you that while he intends to do what he can to assist the inevitable, knowing that what we will do is to oppose the inevitable, what he does and what we do will not be decisive. Destiny will be realized no matter what men do.

There is enough factual support for that dogma taken out of the past decade, from sputnik to Castro, to make it eminently believable on its own grounds to millions of inhabitants of the world today, even apart from the Soviet propaganda machine which carefully accommodates world events, whatever their nature, to this dogma. Make no mistake about it; there is sacrifice in Russia, there is inner discipline in Russia, there is confidence in Russia, there is character of a sort in Russia. The gigantic bootstrap operation which has hurtled Russia ahead in scientific achievements can only be explained as a result of tremendous dedication, not only from the top echelon, but from millions of people who are willing to give up personal pleasure for the sake—at least in part—of the Russian future. Bishop Sheen has seen in this Russian sacrifice and discipline "Christianity without the cross," and in American pleasure-seeking and self-interest, "the cross without Christianity."

If we compare that highly disciplined society, conscious and proud of its achievements and filled with the belief in the truth of its basic dogmas to our own dogma of personal pleasure, then there is reason for alarm.

If you ask me—said George F. Kennan, our distinguished former ambassador to Russia—whether a country with no highly developed sense of national purpose—with an overwhelming accent of life on personal comfort, with a dearth of public services and a surfeit of privately sold gadgetry, without sufficient social discipline—has, over the long run, good chances of competing with a purposeful, serious and disciplined society such as that of the Soviet Union, I must say that the answer is No.

Is Kennan right? Let us look at ourselves through a more distant perspective.

Rome

In the year 1787 mankind stood upon the threshold of the new age. In France the first faint rumblings of the French Revolution could already be heard. In England life was beginning to alter its pace and character under the impact of the Industrial Revolution. And across the seas in America a new country called the United States was just beginning its rise to power. A new age was about to begin, and a spirit ot change and excitement was in the air.

In that same year, in London, after twenty-eight years of intensive research, one of the greatest books in the history of scholarship was finished, *The Decline and Fall of the Roman Empire,* by Edward Gibbon. Why did Gibbon write it?

Because he wanted to know how it happened that the Roman Empire, which was built to last forever, should have crumbled into the dust—and how it was possible for the empire which had the mightiest army, the wisest legal system, the most powerful organization, the finest roads, and the richest culture of all antiquity, to have collapsed. How had a horde of barbarian Huns been able to overthrow it? To find an answer to these questions Gibbon studied every facet of Roman life. And when he was finished with all his research, he reached this conclusion:

Rome was not defeated by the barbarians. By the time they came, her granite walls had already crumbled and fallen from inner decay!

And in the last chapter of the fifth volume, Gibbon summarizes his conclusions by listing the main causes of the collapse of Rome:

The first cause was the corruption of its commerce.

That led to an even greater degree of corruption and immorality among the civil servants, the military leaders, and the government officials.

The spending of more and more public funds on amusements and luxuries instead of essentials. Sports became each year more brutal and exciting, and the public became evermore distracted by the chase after pleasure.

The rapid increase in marital infidelity and divorce brought about the destruction of the home and the family as basic units of society.

The decay of religion as a serious factor in the lives of the people.

One hundred and eighty years have gone by. The new age, which was just beginning when Gibbon wrote his book, is now in full flower. The period that he looked forward to with concern has arrived. Let us, therefore, look at this age of ours carefully with an eye on Gibbon's notes, make a few comparisons, and perhaps learn a lesson.

In many ways, our age is far superior to the Roman Empire.

They built roads which stretched for hundreds of miles: we build rockets that reach to the moon.

They had a powerful infantry: we have weapons which make their spears and swords look like toys.

They had circuses at which a thousand people could be entertained at once: we have television stations that can beam one program to ten million people.

Thus, if you judge by economic power, military might, or technological achievement, our age is a thousand times more developed.

And yet, as we read Gibbon's book and follow in his pages the unhappy description of the gradual decay of the glory that was once Rome, we cannot help but make a comparison between the Roman age and our own.

Gibbon said that the first cause of the collapse of Rome was the *corruption of its commerce.* How does our society stand in the area of its business morality? A study of American business practices has been set forth in *The Operators,* a recent book by F. Gibney. Here are a few typical selections:

According to the United States Better Business Bureau, five billion dollars, which is 1% of the total national product, changes hands each year in bribes, kick-backs and pay-offs!

According to the Bureau of Internal Revenue, one billion, seven hundred thousand dollars was owed the government in 1958 from people who cheated on their income tax. The amount uncollected is estimated at eight billion!

According to the United States Post Office, there was an increase of 29% in the number of mail frauds in three years.

According to National Banking figures, 33% more rubber checks bounced in 1960 (half a billion dollars) than in 1959!

According to the United States Federal Trade Commission, there have been twice as many actions against companies misrepresenting products in 1960 as in 1956!

The above statements include such famous cases as:

The New Jersey company that tripled its price and then gave 15% off.

The Michigan concern which sold secondhand tires as new.

The Pennsylvania gas station that put regular gas into the pumps marked premium.

The Illinois manufacturer who bottled the same product under two different labels, the first guaranteed to grow hair, the second to cure arthritis.

The Swiss watches that were made in Hoboken.

The wonder drug that turned out to be ordinary aspirin.

The British sweaters which were made in Philadelphia from Japanese yarn.

The nationally known cigarette which was finally declared by a government agency to be "not milder."

The book, *The Operators,* lists hundreds of such cases— some beyond the law and some just within the law—cases of double dealing and of deception. It claims, for example, that seventy-five million dollars a year is spent on the campus buying advanced copies of exams, hiring people to write dissertations, or manufacturing fake academic degrees.

Not long ago the entire country was shaken by the television quiz-show scandal. It was hard to believe that Charles Van Doren, son of a leading citizen, had been cheating. It was even harder to believe that almost all of the one hundred and fifty witnesses, who came to testify under oath in court that everything was honest, had been committing perjury. But hardest of all to believe was the fact that, within a few weeks, the shock was over, the country quickly adjusted, a few people were made public scapegoats, and life went back to normal. College students in many campuses filed petitions for Columbia University to reinstate Van Doren as instructor, claiming that the private moral life of a teacher has nothing to do with his career as a teacher. Education, for them, is the accurate transfer of facts and has nothing to do with that old-fashioned goal of molding character, which somehow found its way into the charter of American universities.

One last example from the operators will summarize the moral climate of our society:

> Three men were having lunch together in a very good restaurant. When the bill came, each insisted on paying for it.
>
> —I'm in the eighty per cent bracket, said one, it will cost me twenty per cent.
>
> —Don't be foolish said the second. I'm in the one hundred per cent excess profits bracket and it won't cost me anything.
>
> —I'm on a cost plus contract, said the third as he picked up the bill, I'll make money . . .

This book claims that fraud has become our national pastime. Could it have been worse in Rome?

The second factor that brought about the fall of Rome, according to Gibbon, was the *corruption of the civil servants, the military leaders, and the goverment officials.* How does our society stand in this area?

Two recent events are enough to answer the question of how our society rates in public integrity.

Not long ago, the lurid news broke in Denver of almost unprecedented police corruption (though other cities such as Chicago and New York have been hot competitors). Forty three policemen were implicated in more than two hundred safecrackings over the past ten years, with a total take of two-hundred-fifty thousand dollars. One patrolman, who had become an expert police safecracker, testified:

> A drunk, if he had dough on him, never had it when he got out of jail. If the bartender didn't roll him, the cops did. If the arresting officer didn't roll him, the paddy-wagon did.

On a D. O. A. (Dead on Arrival)—testified another cop, —there's always a race to get there to get the cream. All the cars go. You want to beat the medical examiner and the public administrator, or they'll take it. It's bread.

The wide corruption on the part of both citizens and officials to have made all this possible for such a period of time must have been enormous.

"But everyone is doing it," is the excuse most often given today. And everyone was doing it in Rome, until the walls fell.

The moral laxity of our country and even the lack of patriotism is evidenced in two other widely publicized events. First, of the American prisoners captured in Korea, not one escaped, and many cooperated with the enemy, some even turning to Communism. Extensive government studies reveal the frightening lack of courage and loyalty. The second incident is the continuous work stoppages at missile bases often due to outrageous demands on the part of unions, including one hundred and ten strikes at Cape Kennedy, our missile test center.

"What's happening to our loyalty?"—the Major of the Vandenberg Missile Base asked—"I don't see any evidence of patriotism here. All the workers are looking for is big money. If I tried to reduce overtime pay by putting these guys on eight hour shifts, there would be nobody around in a matter of minutes." After testimony was presented before a Senate Committee, Senator McClellan commented that "wildcat strikes, work stoppages, slow downs, feather-bedding, and a deliberate policy of low productivity on the part of some unions and workers may well be responsible to a substantial degree for whatever lagging behind exists in our space and missile program. If greed, graft and extortion are to dominate our way of life and our economy, especially in a program vital to our survival, it is time for Americans to wake up."

—Reader's Digest

The third factor that led to the fall of the Roman Empire according to Gibbon was the *spending of public money on luxuries instead of essentials.* What are the facts today?

The "facts" are, to put it in terms popularized by Galbraith, that we believe in *private luxury and public poverty.*

We are caught up in a race after luxury and pleasures at all cost. The present philosophy is: private pleasures first, public needs last.

We are fierce balancers of the budget. Every penny must be accounted for, and whatever cannot be defended as an absolute necessity is scrapped when it comes to such "unimportant" commodities as defense, education, public health, city-planning and religion—even though welfare institutions are frightfully under-manned, third rate teachers staff the schools our children attend because they do not receive a living wage, our cities are filthy and transportation poor, and Russia passes us in scientific and military achievement.

But how different is the atmosphere once we turn from public needs to private pleasures? Budgets dare not cramp our style; the sky is the limit; nothing is too good for us when it comes to our own little joys. The new religion which has swept America is neither Billy Graham's Evangelism or California's Zen Buddhism. It is the "cult of the body."

We clothe the body, not so much to protect it from the elements of nature, the heat of the sum, or the wetness of the rain, but simply for the sake of the most recent fashion. We spend precious hours each week in the process of clothing our body. We stock our closets with the latest styles and drain our bank accounts in order to keep up with what advertisers—who shorten and lengthen at will dresses, brims, lapels, etc.—tell us is "smart".

We feed the body, again not so much because of concern for our health or proper nourishment, but more out of desire and pleasure. There are more people who die of overeating in America than of malnutrition. Dieting has become our national pastime. Listen to the conversation at the next party you attend and you will learn that a good portion of it has to do with this or that restaurant, this or that resort, this or that food. And at a time when eighty percent of the three billion people in the world today never had, and never will have, a balanced meal by American standards.

We move the body, not in conveyances proper for our size and weight, but in great, long, sleek cars which have far too much horsepower and can travel far too fast for our normal human needs. There was a time when one horse could pull two men; now we need two- and three-hundred horsepower to move a single man. There are more cars (sixty-two million) than families in America; eighteen percent of the families have two cars. And this at a time when, of the three billion people in the world today, eighty percent never have, and never will, see a doctor.

We satisfy the body, not so much because we are not able to discipline ourselves properly, but because we believe the reason man is unhappy or neurotic or has failed in business or cannot break ninety in golf is because he is inhibited and never gives way to his passions. Satisfy the body and all problems will automatically be solved. But with all our satisfying of our bodily needs, we have not gotten rid of divorce, alcoholism, nor sex problems.

The simple fact of American living is that we are tempted to become faithful followers of the cult of the body, clothing it, feeding it, moving it, and satisfying it, with every luxury money can buy. Paganism has not left us; it rules our lives today more supremely than ever before.

The cult of the body has swept this land of plenty, holding us firmly in its grip, so that we continue to throw a steadily increasing amount of money away on glittering gadgets of all kinds. We live on a fantastically high economic level, devouring our income through the nonsense which the hidden persuaders make us believe we need. Americans spend twice as much each year on vacations as they do on schools. The national average wage of bartenders is twice that of school teachers. The sale of comic books in this country was seven times higher this year than the sale of all text books. The three quarters of a billion dollars spent for church construction last year is more than offset by the half billion that went for pornographic literature. A raise in school taxes was voted down in one community, but the town was able to get permission to issue bond for the construction of a new golf course. John Steinbeck commented:

> If I wanted to destroy a nation, I would give it too much, and I would have it on its knees, miserable, greedy, sick.

The fourth factor which Gibbon lists is the *breakdown of family life*. What is the state of family life in America today?

Twenty-five per cent of New York crime is committed by persons under the age of twenty, and the figure is rising rapidly.

It is estimated that one million illegitimate births occurred last year in our country, double that of only a few years ago.

A Purdue sociologist tells us that one out of six brides is pregnant. (This would explain the present sale of maternity wedding dresses.)

Nearly two million Americans, one-fifth of them teenagers, are estimated by public health authorities to have contracted venereal disease last year, an increase of fifty per cent over the past five years.

"Stealing food from the dorm refrigerator would be more condemned around here," writes a Radcliffe senior, "than fornicating on the living-room couch."

This new sex morality has taken as its banner and its rallying cry, Ernest Hemingway's adage: "What is moral is what you feel good after, and what is immoral is what you feel bad after." On this basis, Norman Peale has pointed out, Hitler could have proved that, for him, slaughtering the Jews was a moral act.

Unbelievable statistics, unbelievable arguments; difficult for parents to accept. More unbelievable by far must be the causes that have contributed to a state of affairs so shocking as to challenge the very institutions of marriage and the family, already considerably shaken by the divorce mortality of one out of every three marriages (that does not mean the other two-thirds are successful):

An easy attitude towards sex.
The collapse of basic moral standards.
The weakening of marital vows.
The growing irrelevancy of religion.

The last cause that Gibbon found for the breakdown of Roman society was the *failure of religion*. When religion degenerated into mere empty form, when it lost its power to serve as a check on the desires of man, when it became a tool for social climbing and an instrument of vanity, Rome was finished.

What is the state of religion in our land today?

In one sense, things have never been so good. More people are joining synagogues and churches today than ever before. Impressive buildings are going up all over the country. It is now socially acceptable, and even socially necessary, to be affiliated with some religious group.

But, if everything else which we have said above so far is true, if this is the moral climate which exists in business, government, and home life, then religion has never been *weaker* than it is today; for religion is evidently unable to serve as a brake on the chase after pleasure, unable to shame the greedy, humble the ambitious or frighten the arrogant. Religion appears to be too easy, too comfortable, too popular to be of any real help in the moral crisis. The "religious boom" has turned out to be a "moral bust."

Communism and the West

In contrast to this drifting pleasure-ride Americans seem to be taking, the Russians have trimmed their personal luxuries down to a minimum, clearly plotted the goals toward which they are moving, and created the discipline of spirit necessary to bring forth both idealism and sacrifice. *Life* magazine, not given to admiring Russian proclamations, had this to say about the Khrushchev manifesto of several years ago on their August 15, 1961, editorial page:

> There are lots of holes in the program, to be sure, and Americans may smile that Khrushchev is promising, as the ultimate goal of Communism, many things we take for granted, such as adequate housing, clothes, shoes and kitchen appliances . . . But it will undoubtedly have an enormous appeal to most Russians who are hungry for a sign of hope. And it will have an undoubted impact on the other big audience it is aimed at—the emerging peoples of new nations who are promised rapid economic and cultural progress that transforms the backward country into an industrial country within the lifetime of one generation, and lifts the people out of darkness.
>
> We can only blame ourselves if we fail to get his chief message to us; total, endless war in which there can be no

final settlement short of our destruction or surrender, a war to which the Russian creed does, indeed, bring a higher order of devotion, of duty (unswerving to Communism) and even of truthfulness—in informing us of our intended fate. Whether or not Russia can fulfill all its grandiose promises, he has put the West at a disadvantage by once again showing the world that Communism *does* have a grand strategy, *does* have a long-range plan that embraces both past and future, can paint its own destiny in terms to convince millions that it *is* history's destined instrument. So saying, it makes us ask: Why has the free world no high powered task force, no combined cold war high command, making equally potent use of their own impressive history of hundreds of millions brought to independence and freedom, of our economic miracles in rebuilding the post-war world, and of master plans to help the emerging nations lift the people out of darkness?

There is a pervasive mood among those vitally concerned with the fate of America, a mood not of defeat, but as of a man who reaches the age when he realizes the dreams of adolescence do not correspond to the realities. How explain the decline of American "prestige" in South America, Africa, Asia, and even in Europe? How explain the propaganda victories of a ruthless Imperialism over the United States in such matters as disarmament and peace, national independence, and anti-colonialism? It is a baffling blow to the pride of this country to see one nation after another turn toward Russian influence, to see the U. N. victories achieved at an ever narrowing margin. Khrushchev predicted that in the near future when we are in the minority, we will treasure the veto as much as Russia does today.

It is in the light of our inner collapse, the gradual weakening of the moral and spiritual foundations upon which American civilization rests, that the rise of Russian Communism as well as its true challenge must be understood. For to conceive of Communism as a military threat alone is to ignore its emergence as a judgment upon the decadence of the West and its appeal as a refuge for those who could no longer bear to look upon that decadence.

Whittaker Chambers, who broke with the Communist party and became one of its most devastating critics, once outlined the power of Communism for a Grand Jury in a New York court by replying to the judge's question: "Mr. Chambers, what does it mean to be a Communist?"

I hesitated for a moment, trying to find the simplest, most direct way to convey the heart of this complex experience to men and women to whom the very fact of the experience is all but incomprehensible. Then I said:

"When I was a Communist, I had three heroes. One was a Russian. One was a Pole. One was a German Jew.

"The Pole was Felix Djerjinsky. He was ascetic, highly sensitive, intelligent. He was a Communist. After the Russian Revolution, he became head of the Tcheka and organizer of the Red Terror. As a young man, Djerjinsky had been a political prisoner in the Paviak Prison in Warsaw. There he insisted on being given the task of cleaning the latrines of the other prisoners. For he held that the most developed member of any community must take upon himself the lowliest tasks as an example to those who are less developed. That is one thing that is meant to be a Communist.

"The German Jew was Eugen Levine. He was a Communist. During the Bavarian Soviet Republic in 1919, Levine was the organizer of the Workers and Soldiers Soviets. When the Bavarian Soviet Republic was crushed, Levine was captured and court-martialed. The court-martial told him: 'You are under sentence of death.' Levine answered: 'We Communists are always under sentence of death.' That is another thing that it meant to be a Communist.

"The Russian was not a Communist. He was a pre-Communist revolutionist named Kalyaev. He was arrested for a minor part in the assassination of the Tsarist prime minister, van Plehve. He was sent into Siberian exile to one of the worst prison camps, where the political prisoners were flogged. Kalyaev sought some way to protest this outrage to the world. The means were few, but at last he found a way. In protest against the flogging of other men, Kalyaev drenched himself in kerosene, set himself on fire and burned himself to death. That also is what it meant to be a Communist."

Whittaker Chambers, *Witness*

* * *

For the first time in our history American prisoners of war in some Korean stockades made no attempt to escape and in several hundred cases turned traitor to their country. Students of the situation inform us that this reflected a lack of understanding on the part of many American troops in combat, and their families back home, as to what America stood for, what task was hers in the world, what, in fact, the basic issues dividing mankind were. Personal security seemed to be—and seems to be—the overwhelming concern. Yet, even in the midst of Western purposelessness, particularly American purposelessness, there have been those who seek a purpose.

The revolutionary heart of Communism—Chambers writes—is not the theatrical appeal: "Workers of the world, unite. You have nothing to lose but your chains." It is a simple statement of Karl Marx, further simplified for handy use: "Philosophers have explained the world; it is necessary to change the world." Communists are bound together by no secret oath. The tie that binds them across the frontiers of nations, across barriers of language and differences of class and education, in defiance of religion, morality, truth, law, honor, the weaknesses of the body and the irresolutions of the mind, even unto death, is a simple conviction: It is necessary to change the world. Their power, whose nature baffles the rest of the world, because in a large measure the rest of the world has lost that power, is the power *to hold convictions and to act on them.* It is the same power that moves mountains; it is also an unfailing power to move men. Communists are that part of mankind which has recovered the power to live or die—to bear witness—for its faith. . . .

What is this faith?

It is not new—continues Chambers—it is, in fact, man's second oldest faith. Its promise was whispered in the first days of the Creation under the Tree of the Knowledge of Good and Evil: "Ye shall be as gods." It is the great alternative faith of mankind. Like all great faiths, its force derives from a simple vision. Other ages have had great visions. They have always been different versions of the same vision: the vision of God and man's relationship to God. The Communist vision is the vision of Man without God.

The Communist atheist vision is clear. Ours is clouded. Is not a people with a vision, even without God, to be preferred to one with no vision at all? Can a people beholding no vision long endure?

The forces of revolution in the West are an intellectual proletariat, disinherited, not in this world's goods with which they are often incongruously replete, but disinherited in the spirit. The revolt of the intellectuals of the West almost without exception begins (no matter how it ends) as the frantic threshing of those drowning in the materialism of the West, a convulsive struggle against the death of the spirit. This is the answer to the fatuous, reiterated question why men like Arthur Koestler or Whittaker Chambers became Communists. For the differences in background, which the shallow world magnifies, are trifling compared to that convulsion of the drowning spirit which carried us, and men like us (each in his own individual way with his own individual rationalization) into Communism, and which makes a second death for those who, recognizing at last that Communism is itself evil, must burst from that second drowning back into a West which has learned nothing and forgotten nothing . . . The West should stop looking at Communism and look into itself. Communism is never stronger than the failure of all other faiths. Men are by nature conservative; they become revolutionists only by despair. Communism did not attract, it repelled me; I became a Communist to escape the dying West.

—Chambers, *Cold Friday*

Will a civilization such as ours, shining without but corroded within, be able to withstand the increasing pressure brought to bear upon it by a force, both purposeful and unprincipled, which patiently moves ahead on many fronts, rolling back not only the prestige of our land but the very spirit of a once proud people?

Will America become another Rome before a new horde of barbaric tribes from the north?

INADEQUATE SOLUTIONS

The world is not ready for nuclear disarmament, or any other kind of disarmament.

—Dr. Edward Teller

In the year 2076 at last the world was ready for disarmament,

And the word went out

And from Asia and the Americas, the delegates, all four of them, came to meet in the stump of a gutted city among degraded Alps.

And the delegates from the Americas said they spoke for the entire population spread out across the hemisphere—perhaps three or four hundred people all told; and that although most of them were sick from disorders of the blood and bone marrow, those who were competent had expressed the wish to ratify the disarmament treaty.

The Asian delegates replied that in behalf of the sovereign people inhabitating the vast land mass between the Baltic and Pacific, amounting to eighty-seven persons including six children, they were equally ready to accept the treaty with only minor qualifications, these to be negotiated before final ratification, but that to all intents and purposes their attitude could be construed as an agreement in principle.

And then the delegates from the Americas asked whether anywhere in the Asias there could be spared any whole milk for the children on their side,

And the Asians replied that though their own needs were sore and pressing, they would be willing to exchange some quarts of whole milk for pints of whole blood, needed for transfusions for the six leukemic children of their own.

The exchange was agreed upon (subject to ratification on both sides of course), but before the conference adjourned two delegates collapsed and died from malnutrition, a third succumbed to sudden virulent infection to which he lacked resistance, and the fourth from internal hemorrhages induced by derangement of the clotting platelets in the blood;

And it was some time before their bodies were discovered, along with the minutes of the meeting. By then the remaining home populations were so weak that the disarmament treaty came into use automatically.

It is still in force today as I, the last human being before my species becomes extinct, write these few words for whatever intelligent beings may chance to visit this planet from dis

—Norman Corwin, *Overkill and Megalove*

Suppose they gave a war and no one came?

(A child's question.)

Therefor hath the curse devoured the earth.

—*Isaiah 24.6*

We cannot continue to live in a situation of paralyzing distrust. If we want to work our way out of the desparate situation in which we find ourselves today, another spirit must enter the people. It can only come if the awareness of its necessity suffices to give us strength to believe in its coming. We must presuppose the awareness of this need in all the peoples who have suffered along with us. We must approach them in the spirit that we are all human beings, all of us, and that we feel ourselves fitted to feel with each other; to think and to will together in the same way. The spirit is a mighty force for transforming things.

—Albert Schweitzer in N. Cousin's *Dr. Schweitzer of Lambarene*

Choose you this day whom you will serve.

—*Joshua 24.14*

—Harry S. Truman said on March 3 President Kennedy "is on the right track" on his decision to resume atmospheric testing. "It was the proper thing to do. We should never have stopped it. Where would we be today if Thomas Edison had been forced to stop his experiments with the electric light bulb?"

—*Washington Star,* March 4, 1962

Why, Harry, we'd be where your father was, reading his
    Bible by gaslight
Or where young Lincoln was, reading law books by the
    glow of a fire in a fireplace
Or where the audience in the Globe was, watching royalty
    carve each other up by lampwick,
Or where Homer was, writing in Greek sunshine.

—Norman Corwin, *Overkill and Megalove*

Judgment is turned away backward
And justice standeth afar off,
For truth is fallen in the street
And equity cannot enter.

—*Jeremiah 23.36*

Cursed be the day
Wherein I was born
The day wherein my mother bore me.

—*Jeremiah 21.14*

4

Inadequate Solutions

I F NEITHER CONTEMPORARY morality nor fear is any guarantee that the bomb will not be used, and if the continual
production of more and better bombs daily increases the possibility of war, what is to be done?

Several solutions have been suggested. Let us consider them.

Military Defense

One suggested solution is military defense.

It has been suggested that America must develop sufficient
military defense to repulse any foreign atomic attacks. The
battle-axe produced the shield, the airplane produced the anti-
aircraft gun, the submarine produced the depth-charge, and
so forth. It follows, then, that we have only to find a satisfac-
tory defense to the new nuclear weapons. Such suggestions are
made with a boldness and certainty probably based more on
arrogance than on knowledge. Pride in one's nation, often a
noble characteristic, is at times stupid in its cocksureness, as
when several summers ago members of the Senate rose in
splendid indignation to denounce any plans for surrender that
our government might be making—or might make in the future!—and, furthermore, voted with admirable anticipation

that no funds be permitted such an un-American project, should such a request *ever* be made! Such deliberations consider everything except the only thing which is really important—the possibility that we may have to surrender.*

The dreadful but necessary counsel of Van Clausewitz, that estimable theorist of modern war, sounds again:

. . . We must therefore familiarize ourselves with the thought of an honorable defeat . . .

It is this kind of pride which has prevented us from understanding the real nature of the Russian threat. It is this kind of pride which allows us to relax on the golf course and play with our gadgets, in confidence that no foreigner can invade our land, no bombs strike our cities, no missiles penetrate our atmosphere, and that somehow or other our Army, our Navy, our Air Force, will protect us as they always have in the past. America has never lost a war, we are reminded.

The time for a rude awakening may be at hand.

*When 'Washington' thinks of 'surrender', it apparently can think only of 'unconditional' surrender. Thus does the demonic specter of the past hover over us, as a still imperious *rector harum tenebrarum.* Thus patriotism, once the last refuge of the scoundrel, now has become the first refuge of the fool. It is folly not to foresee that the United States may be laid in ruins by a nuclear attack; the folly is compounded by a decision not to spend any money on planning what to do after that not-impossible event. There is no room today for the heroic romanticism of the apocryphal utterance. 'The Old Guard dies but never surrenders.' Even Victor Hugo did not put this line on the lips of Cambronne; he simply had him say, 'Merde'. For all its vulgarity, this was a far more sensible remark in the circumstances. For my part, I am impressed by the cold rationality of Soviet military thought as described by Raymond L. Garthoff, *Soviet Strategy in the Nuclear Age* (New York, 1958) : 'The fundamental Soviet objectives which determine political and military strategies may be concisely summarized in one: Advance the power of the Soviet Union in whatever ways are most expedient so long as the survival of the Soviet power itself is not endangered.' For the Soviet Union survival is not an issue in war; for us it is the only issue. In Soviet thought military action is subordinate to political aims; with us military action creates its own aims, and there is only one 'victory,' unconditional surrender. The Soviet strategy concept, in the thermonuclear era as before, is founded on the belief that the primary objective of military operations is the destruction of hostile military forces, and not the annihilation of the economic and population resources of the enemy. Thus contemporary American views often diverge sharply from this traditional stand.' Finally, Soviet policy envisages the 'long war' even after a massive exchange occurs, that is, the end; we have no policy after that, except stubbornly to maintain that it is up to the enemy, and not us, to surrender—unconditionally. There is not little irony in the fact that the communist enemy seems to understand better than we do the traditional doctrine on the uses of force. J. C. Murray, "Theology and Modern War" in *Morality and Modern Warfare.*

We have become so accustomed to thinking of ourselves as militarily impregnable that it is almost second nature for us to continue to do so. The Atlantic and Pacific Oceans have always proved invincible. Wars that we fought were never fought on our soil. We fought on Cuban soil in the Spanish American War; we fought on French and German soil in World War I and again in World War II; later we fought in Korea; now in Vietnam. But must it always be so? It was in fact with these words that the Special Subcommittee on Radiation of the U. S. Congress Joint Committee on Atomic Energy began its report: ". . . For the first time in history American communities have become a part of the main battlefield of a possible war. . . ."

Likewise we have been undefeated in war. But, again, must it always be so? Looking at our wealth and power, our high rate of divorce, juvenile delinquency, murder, and alcoholism, distinguished students of history compare the United States in the middle of the Twentieth Century with the Roman Empire before her defeat by the barbarians from the north. In each case, grand traditions sheltered them, and appear to shelter today, a fatal inner decay. The rise and fall of nations is the law of history. Why should that law change for us? Russia has surpassed us scientifically in several significant areas and boasts she will surpass us economically and technologically in the near future. We may be entering such a turn in the course of history. Historians of civilization are looking toward the decline of the West and the rise of new cultures in the East. To put our hope blindly and foolhardily in military defense is an expression of American pride.

But, to return to the question of military defense itself, the fact remains that *neither at this very moment, nor in the foreseeable future, do we or will we have an effective military defense against nuclear warfare!*

Several years ago nuclear scientist Hans Bethe of Cornell University warned:

> We are entering into a period of mortal peril to all nations with the perfection of intercontinental ballistic missiles. Both the United States and Russia must develop their ICBM's until these missiles become invulnerable.

When that happens the concept of massive retaliation will be reduced to absurdity.

Experts agree that it has happened. Russia already possesses missiles which can accurately reach any point in the United States. There is no magic vault we can erect over our country to insulate it against such messengers of death. No competent military authority will tell us what we wish to hear: that we possess a certain defense against atomic missiles or bombs. And the few shelters extant which can protect against fall-out stand in peril of chemical or bacteriological attack.

Further, the attack may not come through the air at all. There is the possibility that secret agents of a foreign country could bring into the United States parts of the bomb, assemble them in the major cities, and detonate them. The above-mentioned Professor Bethe testified before Congress that the greatest danger to the United States is in smuggling in nuclear bombs.

> Suppose five years from now—he said—thirty nations have nuclear bombs and suppose a hidden bomb should go off in Washington. We would not even know against whom to retaliate. Thus our government's hope of security, massive retaliation, will become meaningless in a few more years.

What about missiles carrying atomic and hydrogen warheads launched by submarines moving up to our very coast beneath water? Admiral Hyman G. Rickover declared:

> It is common knowledge that the Soviets can launch from their submarines missiles with a range of at least 2000 miles. Before too long missiles from submarines will reach any target in the United States.

The United States Navy revealed that the Soviet Union has two hundred ballistic-missile-firing submarines. A further report states that within three years there have been 1,000 sightings of Soviet submarines in the western Atlantic. Senator Jackson declared:

> Our best military intelligence is that the Russians have been working on comprehensive radar charts of the

United States coast lines. This means that a Soviet submarine commander will be able to surface 100 miles off the American coastline, take radar fixes for position and launch his missiles with frightening accuracy.

Furthermore, Soviet submarines are constantly stationed off the United States coastline.

As far back as August, 1959 the Underseas Warfare Advisory Panel to the Military Applications Committee of the Joint Congressional Committee on Atomic Energy released a report which stated:

> . . . the Soviets could mount a devastating submarine nuclear attack against the United States in the 1960's. Our existing defenses could not stop such a missile attack. No weapons system now in existence, even on an experimental basis, offers an adequate defense against non-snorkeling submarines which run quiet and deep.

But perhaps the clearest proof that we have no sure military defense against the bomb is the fact that several important military strategists have soberly advocated an atomic attack on Russia, before she attacks us.

Shelters

A second suggested solution to meet the present emergency, widely proposed not long ago but with less enthusiasm today, is civil defense, the building of fallout shelters which will protect a large proportion of the population in case of war and may even help to prevent one by indicating our readiness. The call from President Kennedy to begin the building of individual shelters touched off a wave of near hysteria in many parts of the country, directing the frustrated concern of millions to seeking safety by burrowing into ground.

Dr. Willard F. Libby, former Atomic Energy Commissioner and one of the leading advocates of shelters, claimed in a newspaper article that "ninety to ninety-five per cent of us [will] survive, with proper protection." This assertion was the occasion for Norman Cousins, brilliant editor of the *Saturday Review*, to make a reply in a series of four editorials.

The logic of his reply was so unrefutable, the attack so devastating, and the implications so far reaching, that it is asserted, government officials, while not admitting it publicly, gradually withdrew from their former shelter policy. Portions of Cousins' statement are reprinted here in some detail.

If this statement [of Libby's that ninety-five per cent can survive] is true, the national debate over shelters ends right here. Any system that can assure protection for at least nine out of ten Americans in a nuclear war is beyond argument.

If on the other hand, the statement is not true, then it clearly represents a profound act of public irresponsibility.

Consider the statement. It stands by itself in the newspaper article. It is not qualified. It does not attempt to correlate the number of casualties with the size and locations of a nuclear attack. It does not make a distinction between an attack directed at military targets and a generalized massive attack directed against population centers. It says nothing about chemical or bacteriological or radiological weapons which, according to the American military, will almost certainly be used in a nuclear war.

It says nothing about firestorms, causing shelters to collapse or converting them into incinerators.

It says nothing about oxygen depletion in shelters during a sustained firestorm.

It says nothing about the time of day an attack might occur. It does not say what would happen if the first wave of an attack came at a time of peak family dispersion, with fathers at work, children at school, and mothers home or in the shops.

It does not deal with the problem of warning time. It does not make known the fact that an adequate alert system does not now exist, or that enough mistakes have already been made in radar detection to emphasize existing imperfections in the system. . . . Dr. Libby as a former member of the U. S. Atomic Energy Commission, is familiar with the estimates of responsible scientists and military experts who contend that a general nuclear

attack involving more than 7,500 megatons could convert
the U. S. into a radioactive wasteland, with or without
shelters.

Does a potential enemy have more than 7,500 megatons
of fission at his disposal? He does. So does the United
States. The total nuclear power available to all nuclear
countries has been estimated to be well in excess of 60,000
megatons and is growing week by week.

Assuming, however, that survival for some is possible for a
variety of reasons:

When the survivors crawl out of their holes they will
not be looking at the world they knew. The crust of the
earth will be burned and clotted; anything that stands,
whether a tree or a structure, will be charred and skele-
tonized. There will be no communications, there will be
no hospitals, there will be no institutions to attend to the
needs of human society. This is what nuclear war is.
No deodorizing can change the fact . . . .

Finally, if the case for shelters has any logic, it should
become a government function. The government should
plan a national program in line with its Constitutional
responsibility. Moreover, if we are to take the need for
shelters seriously, all our plans should be tied to the
absence of warning time. This means that deep (perhaps
400 feet or more) mass underground shelters should be
built from one end of the country to the other. They
should be capable of growing their own food. They
should have practically everything underground we now
have above ground. They should have communications
systems, hospitals, libraries, cultural centers. Most important of all is the fact that we should move into them
immediately, for there will not be enough time to get
into them once the bombs fall.

And what of the terrifying effects of the new shelter men-
tality upon the American public? Cousins continues:

In Las Vegas, the head of the local civil defense agency
recently called for a militia of 5,000 men to protect res-

idents in event of thermonuclear war. The men would be trained to crush an expected invasion—not from foreign shores but from Southern California. It is believed that Los Angeles, as a major city, would be under direct attack. Survivors, warned J. Carlton Adair, the Las Vegas civilian defense official, "would come into Nevada like a swarm of locusts." Obviously, they would have to be repulsed.

In a less organized way, other Americans are now preparing to kill Americans. A Chicago suburbanite, according to *Time* magazine, intends to mount a machine gun at the entrance to his fallout shelter and blast away at shelterless neighbors who might try to get in out of the radioactivity. Countless other Americans may be making no open declarations about their intentions but they are calmly going about the business of equipping their shelters with guns or tear-gas devices, just in case desperate neighbors might want to poach on their preserves during or after an attack. Some are now preparing their children psychologically to accept the murder of their playmates. All this goes under the heading of civil defense.

In Hartford, Connecticut, at a private meeting of local residents who had come together to consider civil defense problems, one citizen advised his neighbors that firearms were standard equipment for shelters, along with stocks of food and medicines. People who are wounded or suffering from radiation will run around like madmen trying to find shelter, he warned. And, since there will be only so much water and food for one's own family, the intruders will have to be turned back even if it means shooting them. A woman who lived next door to the citizen who had just given this advice had a question.

"John," she said, "you and your family have been our closest friends for ten years. Do you mean to say that if this city was bombed and my baby and I were caught in the open, and we were hurt, and came to your shelter, you would turn us away?"

John nodded in the affirmative. His neighbor pressed the point.

"But suppose we wouldn't turn away and begged to get in?"

"It would be too bad," John said, "you should have built a shelter of your own. I've got to look out for my own family."

"But suppose we had built a shelter of our own, yet were caught by surprise, being out in the open at the time of an attack, and we discovered that the entrance to our shelter was covered with rubble and we had no place to turn except to you. Would you still turn us back?"

The answer was still yes.

"But suppose I wouldn't go away and kept trying to get in. Would you shoot us?"

John said that if the only way he could keep his friend out would be by shooting her and her baby, he would have to do it.

In doing so, he could claim spiritual sanction. He referred to a recent issue of an important religious journal which presented a "code of ethics" of Christian morality designed to anticipate difficult questions that might arise in shelters. One point in the code advised the Christians to "think twice before they rashly give their family shelter space to friends and neighbors or to the passing stranger." Finally, the Hartford citizen could cite Civil Defense Coordinator Keith Dwyer's pronouncement that there is "nothing in the Christian ethic which denies one's right to protect oneself and one's family."

People speculate on the horrors that would be let loose by nuclear war. It is not necessary to speculate on such horrors. Some of the worst horrors are already here. The transformation today of otherwise decent people into death calculating machines; the psychological preconditioning for an age of cannibalism; the wholesale premeditation of murder and the acceptable conditions thereof; the moral insolence of those who presume to prescribe the circumstances under which it is spiritually permissible to kill one's neighbors; the desensitization of human response to pain; the acquiescence in the inevitability of disaster; the cheapening of human person-

ality with its concomitant of irresponsible fatalism—all
these are part of an already existing, fast-swelling chamber of horrors.

It will be said that shelters and everything that goes
with them are basic facts of nuclear war that do not disappear because we find them unpleasant. But this assumes there is no alternative. It assumes that everything
has been done to prevent the holocaust from occurring
in the first place.

Diplomacy

A further answer to the peril of atomic war is diplomacy
and international understanding.

Diplomacy and international understanding are necessary
tools in the forging of peace. Unfortunately, we have not
been too successful in manipulating them since the time we
were forced to abandon our traditionally isolationist policy
and to become, along with Russia, a leader in international
affairs.

There have been many schools of thought regarding what
our foreign policy should be toward the Russian threat.
Terms such as "the cold war," "peaceful co-existence," "com-
petitive co-existence" have been employed in describing our
foreign policy attitude toward the Russian threat. But the
most descriptive term for our position was expounded by Mr.
George Kennan, perhaps our most brilliant authority on
Russian affairs, in a now-historic article in *Foreign Affairs* in
1948. He called it "containment." Containment, as expounded
by Mr. Kennan, meant that Russia must be held down,
restrained, by means of a never ceasing pressure—economic
as well as geopolitic, military, and propagandistic—by America
and its allies in the free world. This approach became the
official foreign policy of the United States toward Russia and
has remained so until today. We have ringed Russia with a
series of military bases and have applied pressures which have
at times led us to the very brink of war.

Behind this approach lay two important assumptions:
first, that we must prevent Russia from further expansion,
and, second that containing Russia long enough would cause

her to collapse, because she was weak, her ideology false, her people unhappy, her leaders unstable, her power over-extended, her propaganda nonsense. Rarely have we been as wrong in our estimate of another nation. Russia has grown most impressively, both horizontally and vertically, in the past thirty years.

Vertically, she has sunk her roots in the depth of the human mind, encouraging education on a massive scale, rousing the slumbering senses of the Russian peasants to new life and new achievement, exploring the earth for riches, and mastering the skies with planes and rockets. Scientific development in Russia has been nothing short of phenomenal. Americans were stunned by Sputnik, because that small ball revolving around the earth meant that Russian science, in a hundred important areas, must be further advanced than ours. So stung was American pride that a long overdue revision of our educational system followed. Official international recognition of Russia's vertical achievements—plumbing the earth, dissecting the body, and reaching up to the stars—takes place each year when Russian scientists are awarded Nobel Prizes for their work.

Horizontally, Russia has reached out beyond her millions of square miles to influence the fate of China, Poland, Hungary, Czechoslovakia, East Germany, Cuba and others. Russia speaks successfully to the uncommitted nations through her propaganda, her economic treaties, and her internal agents. Countries that were once within the Western orbit of influence are one by one being lost to that of Russia: first China, then parts of the Middle East, lands in South America, now Cuba, and perhaps Africa. We are shocked when Latin-American countries, whom we have helped, turn against us, when Japan must cancel a presidential visit, and when former "friends" become "neutrals." Such behavior would have been unthinkable in the twenties or even the thirties. The great benefactor—the United States—has now become the great "reactionary," through Russian propaganda, as well as through genuine achievements by Russia, compounded with our own errors.

Our attitude toward Russia today, that is, since the atomic war peril, has had to be totally revised. The old "containment" theory is now quite outdated, and Kennan himself was the first to admit it. It is outdated because its two assumptions—that we can create a Russian stalemate, and that Russia would crumble through internal weakness under a stalemate—have been proved false. The bear sleeps no longer; it has awakened to all its fury. Russia is more vital than we believed, and a stalemate may produce war. A more positive policy—one which will make Russia and the United States partners to an agreement about the bomb is an absolute necessity.

It is the hope of diplomats today that atomic war can be averted through *international agreement*. This is really quite logical, they argue. All states want to abolish atomic weapons. All states declare themselves willing. All thinking people want peace. Everyone is agreeable to renouncing the bomb. We seem so close to a solution. Why, then, do the nations not conclude a treaty and carry out its provisions? Why do they not agree to destroy all existing stockpiles and guarantee that no new ones will be produced? This would be the obvious solution to the problem that confronts us, a way to end the anxiety and torment that beclouds men's minds.

One small obstacle, however, stands in the way—the international inspection! Only if there is international inspection or, to put it in different terms, mutual control, can we have faith in such a treaty. For without such inspection and control what is to prevent our disarming and Russia dissembling disarmament, an old game we have played with nations in the past, except that the stakes are higher this time. Disarmament, then, requires international inspection. But international inspection means that nations must relinquish part of their national sovereignty. And this Russia refuses to do. Thus, the political solution seems both simple and impossible.

As Karl Jaspers has pointed out:

> International control would at once entail consequences going beyond elimination of the atomic threat. International control would inevitably be associated with world-wide change, namely, the transition from a state of affairs in which nations confront one another

like beasts in a jungle, to a community of nations based upon law, whose observance is secured by common institutions. It would mean the transition from a state of mere co-existence which an act of violence can change into war at any moment, to a state of cooperation in which the freedom of all would depend on effective international agreements. This would be the beginning of world peace.

The first consequence of such control would be that the powers would gain insight into all aspects of all situations, which must of itself lead to mutual frankness, and finally to the collective spirit indispensable for peace.

The second consequence of control would be the voluntary restriction of state sovereignty by treaties, whose enactment, as with all laws, must not be based on trust alone, but on an effective controlling agency. Such an agency would be set up by the contracting parties themselves. Only in this way can the freedom arbitrarily to violate treaties be eliminated. The setting up of such a mutual international control would mark the first and probably crucial step toward a situation in which the atom bomb could, with relative certainty, be ruled out. For the atom bomb can be abolished with certainty only if war as such is made impossible.

Jaspers goes on to outline what, in his opinion, would constitute the political principles upon which world peace might be based:

(1) Treaties are recognized as legally binding, unless they are changed by new negotiations. Even in the event of profound differences of opinion, the verdict of legal agencies is to be accepted. But just as the state cannot abolish its police force, so the peaceful international order cannot renounce all use of force. How to constitute an international police force under the control of the supreme legal authorities, is one great problem.

(2) The supremacy of law requires renunciation of absolute sovereignty. This implies that the decisions of the appointed officials would be determined by a majority

of votes and that the right to veto would be renounced. Instead, it should be possible, after a lapse of time, to submit every verdict of the judicial authorities to review new negotiations and eventual revision. The setting up of supernational officials, appointed by the states and endowed with such unprecedented great powers, is the second problem.

(3) The actual conclusion of peace implies unrestricted exchange of news reports, and free and public confirmation of ideas, without any censorship in either instance. The achievement of a change for the better requires world-wide publicity.

(4) The nations will be concerned with each other's internal affairs. Injustice must be condemned by the whole world. Reparation of internal wrongs—for instance, when human rights are violated—would be possible through international courts.

(5) Unjust political divisions and treaties, originating in the past, would be subject to revision. Subjugated nations are to be freed, if they so desire, by an international agency. Free and secret ballots are the means for ascertaining the people's will.

—K. Jaspers, "The Atom Bomb and the Future of Man," *Evergreen Review.*

Jaspers has here endeavored to explore what lies beneath "mutual inspection," namely, that a broad international base of cooperation between nations is required to really achieve our goal. International law, renunciation of veto, surrender of national sovereignty—these are some of the steps that must be taken. It is precisely because Russia is aware of all of this that she refused to permit inspection of her country by other nations. And even if Russia suddenly agrees to mutual inspection, it is the broader base of cooperation which is vital and which, if not entered into, will make such inspection unworkable. At the moment we are at a standstill. Our diplomats are working toward abolishing the

bomb and setting up international controls, but Russia resists. The blueprint for world peace is clear, but Russia
will have no part of it.

And how far will diplomacy get us with China, who openly
proclaims as its goal the conquest of America, and whose
scientists have already exploded their first atomic bombs?

To put the paradox more concisely:

In view of the H-bomb, war should be obsolete. But it is
not!

In view of the H-bomb, nationalism—national sovereignty—
should be obsolete. But it is not!

The solution to atomic war through *international agreement* which at first seemed the sensible way, now appears
no more certain than solution through *military defense*.

DIVINE INTERVENTION

Seattle—Russian cosmonaut Gherman Titov proclaimed Sunday, April 5, 1962, his disbelief in God
and said he saw "no God or angels" during his 17
orbits of the earth. . . . "Some people say there is a
God out there," the 27-year-old Soviet major [said],
"but in my travels around the earth all day long I
looked around and didn't see him. I saw no God
or angels. No God helped build our rocket. The
rocket was made by our people."

(A.P. report from Seattle)

When reached for comment, God said:

Unfortunately I missed the orbiting of Cosmonaut Titov,
which should not be held against me, since the Russians
made no advance public announcement of his flight.

At the time I was busy elsewhere creating a new sun
roughly similar to your own, distant by a great many
of what you call parsecs, from the scene.

No slight was intended.

The absence of angels is simply explained:

They were busy protecting the Chairman of the Party,
the one who kisses returning Cosmonauts. There is a
large vein in the region of his right temple which could
pop under strain or upon hard drinking, and all the
angels in the region who could be spared that day were
helping him resist temptation, as assigned.

May I add, it is perfectly true I had no hand in building
the rocket. It was, as the major said in Seattle, made
by his people.

It was not the rocket I made, only the people.

—Norman Corwin, *Overkill and Megalove*

It is our temptation to assume that, because our opponents are atheists, God must be on our side and to over-
look the extent to which Communism is a judgment upon
the sins and failures of the middle-class world, upon the
Christian world. The very atheism of Communism is a

judgment upon the churches which for so long were unconcerned about the victims of the industrial revolution and early capitalism and which have usually been ornaments of the *status quo,* no matter how unjust it has been.

—John C. Bennett

Woe unto you that desire the day of the Lord!
Wherefore would ye have the day of the Lord?
It is darkness, and not light.
As if a man did flee from a lion,
And a bear met him;
And went into the house and leaned his hand on the
    wall,
And a serpent bit him.
Shall not the day of the Lord be darkness, and not light?
Even very dark, and no brightness in it?
The end is come upon My people Israel;
I will not again pardon them any more.
And the songs of the palace shall be wailing in that day,
Saith the Lord God;
The dead bodies shall be many;
In every place silence shall be cast.
Hear this, O ye that would swallow the needy,
And destroy the poor of the land,
Shall not the land tremble for this,
And everyone mourn that dwelleth therein?
And it shall come to pass in that day,
Saith the Lord God,
That I will cause the sun to go down at noon,
And I will darken the earth in the clear day.
And I will turn your feasts into mourning,
And your songs into lamentation;
And I will make it as the mourning for an only son,
And the end thereof as a bitter day.

Behold, the days come, saith the Lord God,
That I will send a famine in the land,
Not a famine of bread, nor a thirst for water,
But of hearing the words of the Lord.

(Amos 5:18-20, 8:2-11)

Father, what am I to answer those people who keep writing me that I was wrong to write in *Witness* that I had left the winning side for the losing side? They say that by calling the West the losing side, I have implied that evil can ultimately overcome good.

Father Alan studied his hands, which were lying in his lap. Then he glanced at me directly and asked: "Who says that the West deserves to be saved?"

If, in that softly lighted room, Father Alan had burst a Verey flare, he could scarcely have lit up more effectively the ravaged landscape of that No Man's Land across which the West confronts its crisis, supposing that it is only an alien enemy it confronts, not knowing that the enemy it confronts is first of all itself.

Whittaker Chambers, Cold Friday

A fire is kindled in mine anger,
And shall burn unto the lowest hell,
And shall consume the earth with her increase,
And set fire to the foundations of the mountains.

(Deut. 32:22)

For, behold, the day cometh,
That shall burn as an oven;
And all the proud and all that work wickedness,
Shall be as stubble.

(Mal. 3:19)

5

Divine Intervention

There are others who assert that if human might and mind—military defense and international agreement—cannot prevent atomic destruction, *God* can! Surely He will not permit the creature He fashioned and placed upon this earth, who was made in His image and to whom He gave lordship over the entire earth, to be destroyed.

This is an argument that many of us toy with when all else begins to crumble. We like to consider it, rest upon it, embrace it—because it is reassuring.

But are we so sure that God wants to save us? Are we so confident that we *deserve* being saved?

Who dares declare that he knows the will of God? Perhaps He has had enough of us, disgusted with our killings, our hating, our wars, our treachery, our intrigue, our concentration camps and gas chambers, our Bergen Belsens and Treblinkas, our Cains and Hamans, our Ghengis Khans and Attilas, our Hitlers and Stalins, our miserable struggle for money and power and ego-satisfaction, with the filth and rottenness of our world and our lives. Perhaps He thought that the human race might learn in time from the suffering and tragedy which it encountered in the world and would, thereby—in a hundred years, a thousand years, three thousand years—become faithful to Him. But we did not. Each new generation repeats the follies of those who have gone before, until the demon of darkness prevails.

Eichmann

It is not easy to argue the merits of man after the searing, systematic evidence of the trial of Adolph Eichmann, the *locus classicus* of the decline and fall of *homo sapiens*. That trial portrayed as never before the distortion of God's image into an incredible monster. The rising tide of blasphemy which has been slowly seeping into the human spirit over the centuries, banishing pity and justice and crying the cry of the old pagan gods—blood and might and death—but in a voice modulated by Heidelberg chemists and Berlin psychologists—suddenly burst forth in its demonic frenzy for all to see. Public display was made of the horror that inhabits the human soul, raising the terrible question of this creature's right to anything, even continued existence.

For that was not just a trial like other trials. It was an expedition beyond the accursed underworld of a Dostoievsky or the boiling waters of Dante's pit, not a journey into that hell which may await us in a world beyond but into one which already ensnares us in this world. A journey into that cellar of the soul, that hell of the human heart beside which the purposeless terrors of nature—fire, storm, earthquake, wild beasts—are as naught. For three months, documented testimony, eye-witness accounts, films made by the Nazis themselves, and carefully accumulated evidence relating to history's most hideous crime were presented through mass media to an audience comprised of most of the nations of the earth. This was the Eichmann trial. Evil incarnate, for the present at least, will be associated with that inquiry, not because the list of human monstrosities ends or begins here, but because never before has evil so infernal been perpetrated on such a scale, and never before has the world been made to stand witness, testifying not only to man's actions but questioning his very existence.

What was some of the "evidence" of the trial?

A father told how he had been forced to throw the bodies of his son and daughter on the crematory fires.

Husbands were compelled to have sex relations with other men's wives in view of their children.

In Terezin every Friday at least one hundred people—not all Jews—would be crammed into a tiny cell, cell thirty-eight, children too. In the morning they would be dead and dragged out with a special long fork curved like animal's teeth. Thursday night was S.S. rape night in the third ward, the Jewess's cell. Even through the massive masonry their screams could be heard. Any who resisted were shot.

Nazi soldiers delighted in testing their revolver marksmanship by aiming at the tips of Jews' fingers and noses.

Starvation led inmates to acts of cannibalism.

Once at Majdanek children were treated with kindness— each was handed a sweet at the entrance to the gas chambers.

Babies were hurled into the air and caught at the end of bayonets in the presence of their mothers.

A German loudspeaker played cradle-songs while children were separated from their parents to be sent to extermination camps.

The Jews were buried methodically, head and feet being alternated to save space in the mass graves.

Mothers were lashed away from their children with whips. One mother refused to be parted from her baby, and an S.S. man snatched it from her and smashed the child's head on the ground. He handed the child to the mother and said: "Now take your child."

Prisoners were used as guinea pigs for "scientific" research by highly trained German scientists: how long a human being could tolerate cold water, lack of oxygen and the effect of various deadly germs were observed and recorded with efficient precision. We possess the records.

A letter Eichmann received from Professor Hirt, Chief of Anatomical Institute of Strasbourg University:

> Subject: Securing skulls of the Jewish-Bolshevik commissars for the purpose of scientific research at the Reigh University at Strasbourg.
>
> We have a large assembly of skulls of nearly all races and peoples at our disposal. Of the Jewish race, however, only a few specimen skulls are available. . . . The war in

the east gives us a chance of putting this right. By obtaining the skulls of the Jewish-Bolshevik commissars who represent the prototype of the repulsive, but typical, sub-human, we have now the chance to obtain scientific material.

Following the killing of the Jew, whose head should not be damaged, the physician will separate the head from the body and will forward it to its proper point of destination in a hematically sealed tin can especially made for this purpose and filled with preservative fluid. The comparison tests and anatomical research on the skull, as well as the determination of the race membership and of pathological features of the skull form, the form and size of the brain, etc., can be undertaken by photographs, measurements, and other data supplied on the head and skull itself.

Nazi films showed the inside of gas chambers, occasionally fixing on the dark openings from which lethal gas poured down upon millions of victims. Other pictures portrayed the burying of bodies in the open when the jammed crematoria could not accommodate the flow of gassed bodies. One scene showed a transport of tiny children, some of them barely reaching to the tops of the polished boots of the S.S. men herding them into gas chambers.

One of the films showed heaps of glasses, gold teeth, a mound of babies' shoes, heaps of hair shorn from woman victims before gassing, and then huge reams of cloth woven from the hair. In another, thousands of naked men and woman marched in deep snow before S.S. guards. There were pictures of headless bodies laid out in neat rows like sardines and next to them barrels of heads. This scene was filmed at the Institute for Racial Research at Strasbourg.

Another witness, a member of a detail which carried bodies from the gas chamber, testified that about four hundred Jews were pushed at bayonet point into each gas chamber. At one time, when all chambers were working, ten thousand victims were gassed simultaneously within forty-five minutes. The gas was emitted from special diesel engines operated by two Ukranians whose names the witness knew only as Ivan and

Nikolai. He testified that at first horrible cries were heard which died into moans and finally silence. Afterwards, the S.S. men called out "all are sleeping," and the bodies were then taken to mass graves. Children who fell from their mother's arms and who remained alive on the floor of the gas chambers were shot by the S.S. men and the Ukranians. He said that after the first day of this terrible work, many members of his group committed suicide.

A witness told the court that Mengele, nicknamed "the angel of Death," regularly chose boys for the gas chambers. He said that the method used on one Yom Kippur Eve was particularly grim. About two thousand boys were ordered to assemble on a field. Mengele selected a taller boy and nailed a strip of wood to a post to indicate his height. The other boys were then ordered to measure themselves by the marker. Everyone understood that boys shorter than the marker would be sent immediately to death. Half of the two thousand boys were gassed. The general feeling in the camp, the witness said, was that the Nazis chose Yom Kippur for the murder of the boys with knowledge of the Yom Kippur prayer, *"Unesaneh Tokef,"* which describes all mankind as passing under God's staff, with Mengele demonstrating that he was the one who decided who should live and who should die.

A German civilian engineer testified to the following:

An old woman with snow-white hair was holding a one-year old child in her arms and singing and tickling it. The child was cooing with delight. The parents were looking on with tears in their eyes. The father was holding the hand of a boy about ten years old and speaking to him softly; the boy was fighting his tears. The father pointed towards the sky, stroked the boy's head and seemed to explain something to him. At that moment the S.S. man at the pit shouted something to his comrade. The latter counted off about twenty persons and instructed them to go behind the earth mound. The family I have described was among them.

I well remember a girl, slim and with black hair who, as she passed me, pointed to herself and said: "Twenty-three years old." I then walked around the mound and found myself confronted by a tremendous grave. People were closely wedged together and lying on top of each other so that only their heads were visible. Nearly all had blood running over their shoulders from their heads. Some of the people shot were still moving. Some lifted their arms and turned their heads to show that they were still alive. The pit was already two-thirds full. I estimated that it held a thousand people. The people—they were completly naked—went down some steps which were cut in the clay wall of the pit and clambered over the heads of those who were lying there to the place to which the S.S. men directed them. They laid down in front of the dead and wounded. Some caressed the living and spoke to them in a low voice. Then I heard a series of shots. I looked into the pit and saw that their bodies still twitched or that their heads lay motionless on top of the other bodies before them. I looked for the man who did the shooting. He was an S.S. man who sat at the edge of the narrow end of the pit, his feet dangling into it. He had a tommy gun on his knees and was smoking a cigarette.

—C. Clarke, *Eichmann*

Film scenes were shown of Germans brought back to camp, following their capture after liberation, so that they might look on what they had done. They walked gingerly among the dead, holding handkerchiefs to their noses to avoid the unpleasant smell of the charnel-houses they had created and operated.

Yehiel Dinur, who wrote *The House of Dolls* under the pseudonym, "Ka-tzenik 135633," testified. "Ka-tzenik" is a hebrew abbreviation for concentration camp inmates, while the number represents the identification number tatooed by the Nazis on his arm. Dinur began by replying to a question from the prosecution as to why he had chosen the pseudonym rather than using his own name. He said:

I did not see myself as a writer of literature but only as one recording impressions I cannot suppress and cannot forget. I was in Auschwitz about two years. Time there wasn't like time is measured here. There every fraction of a minute revolved on wheels of another time measurement. We had no names, no parents, no children. We did not wear things as things are worn here. We didn't live, we didn't die. The rules there were not rules of this earth. Our names were numbers.

At this point, the witness rolled up the sleeves of his jacket to show his number. He continued: "We were on another planet called Auschwitz." Then, he displayed the striped pajama-type garb worn by Auschwitz inmates. He handed the garment to the prosecution to submit as an exhibit. Correspondents who were able to pull their gaze away from the witness said later that both Eichmann and Servatius turned pale. The three judges held their breath and a deep sigh arose from the audience. The witness spoke again:

> I believe with perfect faith—he said this in the Hebrew of Maimonides used frequently by Orthodox Jews at the end of the daily prayer—that I have to carry on under this pseudonym as long as the world fails to react to the crucifixion of our nation to eradicate this evil. If I stand before you and relate what happened on this planet, if I could be heard now, then I believe with perfect faith that this is due to a solemn oath that gave me this strength. This oath was my armor. It girded me with superhuman strength during the two years at Auschwitz. This oath was—to chronicle should I survive.

At this point the witness, who was in his forties, collapsed.

Who was on trial?

At a closed meeting of distinguished editors of the American religious press which I attended, the then impending Eichmann case was presented for discussion. One by one these writers and thinkers raised objections: objections to the manner of apprehension ("kidnapping"), to the place of the trial ("a prejudiced court," "Israel was not in existence when the crimes were committed") and to the type of punishment ("better to act with mercy"), concluding that "it is questionable whether any moral lesson could be derived from immoral acts." Only after soul-searching hours of discussion did it dawn upon some of the discussants that the real meaning of the Eichmann trial was that *they too* were on trial beside him, and that their initial reaction had unwittingly evidenced the kind of moral quibbling which made an Eichmann possible.

As the trial proceeded, the transformation which took place in the above discussion, was repeated in different parts of the world. Several things became clear: (1) that no other nation wanted to put Eichmann on trial, (2) that the court was eminently fair, (3) that the punishment was irrelevant, and (4), strange as it may seem, that Eichmann was the least important person in the courtroom. He had become the occasion for the documentation and revelation to the world—through newspapers, television, radio, movies, plays, novels and serious studies—of the Nazi crime against the Jews. And each time a ghastly report of inhumanity was made, listeners and readers all over the world paused and asked themselves a question they could not answer—

"How could it have happened?"

For along with Eichmann in his bulletproof glass cubicle there sat others who were also on trial in that Jerusalem courtroom.

The German businessmen who engaged in lively competition to procure orders for building the death machines were on trial.

The firm of I.A. Topf and Sons of Erfurt, manufacturers of heating equipment, was on trial. A letter from the firm dated Feb. 12, 1943 reads:

> To the Central Construction Office of the S.S. and Police, Auschwitz:
>
> *Subject*: Crematoria 2 and 3 for your camp.
>
> We acknowledge receipt of your order for five triple furnaces, including two electric elevators for raising corpses and one emergency elevator. A practical installa-

tion for stoking coal was also ordered and one for transporting ashes.

The C. H. Kori Company was on trial. For we have in our possession the carefully filed correspondence in which is recorded their pride in constructing furnaces for Dachau and Lublin which

> have given full satisfaction and proven efficient and operational in practice. Following our verbal discussion regarding the delivery of equipment of simple construction for the burning of bodies, we are herewith submitting plans for the perfected cremation ovens which operate with coal and which have hitherto given full satisfaction. We suggest two crematoria furnaces for the building, but we advise you to make further inquiries to make sure that two ovens will be sufficient for your requirements. We guarantee the effectiveness of our cremation ovens as well as their durability, the use of the best materials, and our faultless workmanship.

The seven archbishops of Austria in 1938 were on trial. On the first Sunday after Hitler's victorious entrance into Vienna at the head of his forces, these representatives of the countries conscience who had watched the rise of the Nazis in Germany at close range, published a proclamation of welcome which was posted at every corner in the city and read from every church:

> Our thousand year longing for unification with the German people has now been achieved. We joyfully recognize the Nazi movement that has produced these wondrous achievements. We call upon all faithful Christians to take cognizance of what they owe to their nation.

The Pope was on trial. President Roosevelt instructed his Ambassador in Italy to request a statement from Pope Pius XII condemning Nazi persecution of the Jews, and Cordell Hull, then Secretary of State, himself appealed. The negative reply included this reason: that the Pope had already expressed his disapproval and, furthermore, that the crimes had not been substantiated. I am not aware that any Nazi Catholics, including Hitler, were excommunicated.

The Czech Minister of the Interior in that same year, 1938, was on trial with Eichmann. For on March 12 the last train fleeing from Vienna contained three hundred enemies of Nazism, with passports, expecting to be interned in the neighboring democracy, Czechoslovakia. Instead they were met with bayonets which turned their train back to Vienna and death.

On trial with Eichmann was President of the Swiss Red Cross who did not press his right to enter the concentration camps, and when at last in 1944 he did visit Auschwitz, his recommendation was for food parcels!

The British head of the Near East was on trial with Eichmann. When Joel Brandt reached Turkey toward the end of the war with the report that Eichmann offered one million Jews for ten thousand loaded trucks, he was sent to Cairo and imprisoned by the British Minister whose reply to the offer was, "A million Jews! What would we do with a million Jews?"

The Allied countries were on trial as well. Those who refused to accept Jewish immigrants unless they possessed visas from the people who sought to murder them; those who ignored frantic requests to bomb the railroads going to Auschwitz but bombed "vital" areas nearby; those who closed their doors to immigrants who had nowhere to go; those whose high priorities did not include an effort to halt the "final solution."

And, finally, Christianity was on trial. For two thousand years Christians had looked back to a trial which took place in Jerusalem and held guilty a people whose alleged involvement they found conclusive. Now in that same city, Jerusalem, another man was tried, a Christian, and beside him the shadow of Christiandom's failure in the modern world.

The sins of Christianity were two. The first was silence of the spirit before all the hells of Satan—a silence which the young German playwright, Rolf Hochhuth, has placed at the center of a brilliantly lit stage for all the world to gaze upon

in shock unbelieving, in tears unending, and in repentance
unremitting.

> For sixteen months now Rome has known
> what Hitler is doing to Poland: why does
> the Pope say not one word about it?
> There where the towers of his churches stand,
> stand also Hitler's smoking chimneys.
> Where the bells ring on Sundays,
> the ovens burn on weekdays:
> that is the look of the Christian West today.
> Why, Eminence, should God
> not send another flood?
> Only the tanks of Stalin are now able
> to free Treblinka, Auschwitz, Majdanek . . .
> . . . the King of Denmark, a defenceless man,
> threatened Hitler he would wear the star,
> along with *every member* of his house,
> if the Jews in Denmark were
> forced to do so . . . They
> were not forced. When, finally,
> will the Vatican act so that
> it will be possible once more for a priest
> to admit without shame that he
> is a servant of *that* Church, which sees
> in brotherly love its first commandment? . . .

—R. Hochhuth, *The Deputy*

The second sin of Christianity was seeking salvation of souls
instead of deliverance of human beings. Reverend William
Hull, an American clergyman, was appointed spiritual ad-
visor to Eichmann before his execution and recorded his visits
with him in an effort to convert him.

> Hull: . . . please turn to *Ecclesiastes 12:4.*
> Eichmann: Is that in the Old Testament?
> Hull: Yes.

Eichmann: I will not read the Old Testament; it is nothing but Jewish stories and fables. I refuse to read them. . . .

Hull: "Jesus said, Render therefore unto Caesar the things which are Caesar's; and unto God the things that are God's." I look upon capital punishment as entirely a legal matter, outside the province of the church. . . .

Jesus said, "Be not afraid of them that kill the body, and after that have no more than they can do. But . . . Fear Him, which after he hath killed hath power to cast into Hell . . . Fear Him." My interest primarily is in the soul of a man, rather than in his body. If a man's soul is prepared and ready, what then is death but an ushering in to a much better life. . . .

We told you once that you will not be judged for your deeds. Your judgment will be based on your faith and only on your faith. The only basis of God's judgment is whether you believe in Jesus Christ and have faith in Him . . .

     —William L. Hull, *The Struggle for a Soul*

After the execution, Hull was interviewed in Canada:

Question: Suppose Eichmann had re-accepted Jesus?

Hull: Then he would have immediately entered Paradise without passing through purgatory at all.

Question: Though he had murdered 6,000,000 Jews?

Hull: If he accepted Jesus before his execution, he would thereby have been cleared of his guilt, since, according to Christian doctrine, Jesus had by his own blood atoned for all the sins, past and future, of all men who accept Him.

Question: And what about the souls of his 6,000,000 Jewish victims?

Hull: They certainly did not enter Paradise, but were consigned to Hell, because they died without accepting Jesus as their Saviour. Without acceptance of Jesus, there is no salvation.

Henrich Heine, the nineteenth-century German poet, was one of the few whose troubled eye had pierced the veil of the future. He wrote:

> Christianity—and this is its noblest merit—mitigated in a measure that brutal Germanic lust for war; it could not destroy it, however. Should the taming talisman, the cross, shatter some day, there will then burst forth again the ferocity of the old warriors, the insane frenzy of which the Nordic poets sing and speak so much. The talisman is decaying and the day will come when it will woefully break down. The old stone gods will then rise from the long-forgotten ruins, rub the thousand-year-old dust from their eyes, and Thor with his giant sledge hammer will, in the end, leap forth and smash the Gothic cathedrals.

Even Heine, however, was unable to foresee that the breeding ground of the new man-beast would not be limited to Germany alone, but would spring up as an uncontained epidemic of destruction in many countries. The defeat of the Nazis has meant neither the defeat of Nazism and Fascism nor a quieting of the spirit of inhumanity with which they were imbued. It has not meant the elimination of the man-beast, spawned in the muck of the corrupted soul, which is the legacy of our time. This hydraheaded monster replaces one lost limb with ten new ones. Instead of one Hitler we now have ten tyrants—none, perhaps, so demonic at the moment, but all potentially his like. The present Communist menace is as fearful as the past Nazi menace. The new man-beast seeks to embrace the entire world in its satanic grip of hate and death.

Compassion shuns our world. There has been so much cruelty and suffering that the senses have become dulled; so much spilled blood that its sight no longer frightens us; so many rotted bodies that their stench no longer sickens us. The worst horror is that there is no horror. Where were the democratic nations, our allies and friends, and where was our own land of liberty and freedom, when human beings were being slaughtered in the charnel houses of Europe? Where

were many of us? Do not think that we have remained un-
affected by the cruelty of our times. Our feelings, too, have
been ravished by the disease.

The death of God or man?

Nietzsche, more than a century ago, proclaimed the glorious
new epoch of man, liberated from self-imposed restraints which
had shackled his noble instincts, with words that have echoed
down the corridors of modern literature and thought until
they became the foundation for new philosophies and, ultimately, political action:

> Have you not heard of that mad man who lit a lantern
> in the bright morning hours, ran to the market place, and
> cried incessantly, 'I seek God! I seek God!' As many of
> those who do not believe in God were standing around
> just then, he provoked much laughter. 'Why, did he get
> lost?' said one. 'Did he lose his way like a child?' said
> another. 'Or is he hiding? Is he afraid of us? Has he
> gone on a voyage? Or emigrated?' Thus they yelled and
> laughed. The mad man jumped into their midst and
> pierced them with his glances.
>
> 'Where is God!' he cried. 'I shall tell you. We have
> killed him—you and I. All of us are his murderers. There
> has never been a greater deed! And whoever will be born
> after us—for the sake of this deed he will be a part of a
> higher history than all history hitherto. What are the
> churches now if they are not the tombs and sepulchers of
> God! God is dead. God remains dead. And we have
> killed Him!'

That childlike illusion of the divine which distorted the
glory of man's natural desires was to be swept away; all religious fetish and superstition, invented by the weak in order to
chain the strong in violation of the only law of life, the survival of the fittest, was to be cast off. Freeing himself from the
shackles of faith, man would now emerge from his stunted
existence and rise to that full human stature which nature had
intended him from the very beginning. "Glory to man in the

highest," wrote Swinburne in 1875, "the maker and master of things."

The unthinkingly shallow heard in that cry—"God is dead!"—the wildest blasphemy, and the unthinkingly intelligent heard it as a stupid promise of emancipation. But Nietzsche was only reading aloud the transcript of his time. That time comes whenever men remake God so much in their own image that He no longer corresponds to reality.

It was the doctrine of progress, the assumption of inevitable improvement, which formed the boundaries of modern man's thinking for more than a century. The Darwinian doctrine of biological evolution was used to explain human society— something Darwin himself never intended. Events seemed to confirm this point of view. Where there were formerly mounds of rubble, now great steel and glass cities sprang up. Turbulent rivers were spanned by magnificent bridges. The skies were conquered, the mountains climbed, the depths of the earth plumbed. Soon, they believed, socialism, democracy, universal education, science, and human reason would create a utopian society which would bring about that universal brotherhood of which all mankind had dreamed.

So Victor Hugo could write that "by the end of the nineteenth century, war will be dead, the scaffold will be dead, hatred will be dead, frontiers will be dead, royalty will be dead, dogmas will be dead—and man will begin to live."

But here we are half way through the twentieth century, and war is not dead, the scaffold is not dead, hatred is not dead, frontiers are not dead, royalty is not dead, dogmas are not dead—but *man* is beginning to die.

The nineteenth century proclaimed the death of *God;* the twentieth century announced the death of *man.*

Dehumanization—the gradual suffocation of modern man's soul—has no more ghastly example, in its final grisly stage, than he who was on display before all the world in a bullet-proof glass cubicle in Jerusalem—Eichmann!

Dehumanization means, in part, absence of a sense of guilt. Eichmann sat through that trial, during which the accounts of horrors of Nazi persecution of Jews made even hardened reporters weep like children, with a sense of quiet calm. When movies were shown so frightful that few had the courage to look at them, he scrutinized each detail, carefully jotting down his endless comments. Never was there a clear-cut confession, a heartbroken cry of repentance, a humble admission of responsibility. Nor were there at Nuremberg.

Perhaps the key to the entire trial was, when the judge asked Eichmann what he considered of the highest importance, he answered: to obey orders. Thus he absolved not only himself, but all Nazis who had committed the horrors, from responsibility. He was only obeying orders. All Nazis were only obeying orders. The privates obeyed the captains, the captains obeyed the generals, and the generals obeyed Hitler. Only one man was responsible for all the terror and bloodshed and murder. All others were innocent.

Men who had incinerated fellow humans lived without guilt.

If to be human is to be responsible as Genesis teaches, for Cain was turned "outcast and fugitive" from the abode of men, because he was not responsible, felt no guilt, did not hear the voice of conscience; if man is "responsible consciousness" as one modern philosopher has defined him, and it is this which in essence differentiates him from the beast, then was Eichmann a man? Can one who no longer knows guilt, feels responsibility, or hears the voice of conscience still be called a man? He looked like a man, spoke like a man, dressed like a man, but was he not in truth something less than a man—a dehumanized beast?

Eichmann does not stand alone. He is a symbol of the dehumanization which has taken place and is taking place in totalitarian lands which now embrace perhaps a billion human beings who are trained to recognize good and evil, right and wrong, justice and injustice only insofar as they relate to the will of the state. That palace of kindness, morality and sensitivity, which has been cultivated with infinite sacrifice century after century—the human being—is hardly recognizable. Our age differs from others which have gone before in that not only cities and nations have been conquered, but man himself is being done away with. Man is dying. Only the beast may remain.

What was revealed at the Eichmann trial was the ultimate paradigm of man sundered from God. For, as Dostoievsky has taught us: "If there is no God, anything is permitted."

"As a tree torn from the soil, as a river separated from its source, the human soul wanes when detached from what is greater than itself (Heschel)."

Man is part beast and part angel. When he forgets the angel within him and the heavens above him, his spirit grows sick, for there is nothing to draw him upward and beyond, nothing to carry him forward, and he slips downward into the clutches of what lies hidden in the depths of his soul. Man is not an automonous being who created himself and sprang to full stature from the dust of the earth, independent of all else, reliant on no one else. In the pride of his achievements, when he parades the fascinating gadgets he has fashioned and beholds the tinsel splendor of empires and glory, he may well believe that he needs no guide, no will, no source beyond the genius of himself. But when this happens—and this is what has and is happening before our eyes—then man becomes something less than man, his spirit withers, and the beast within him gains in the struggle for the mastery of his soul. For we are attached at the root of our soul to One Who is greater than all our wisdom, all our genius, all our creations, and from Whose source the power of life flows. Forget that source, cut ourselves loose from that guidance, and we begin to decay and grow weak in heart, overcome by all the terrors of history.

Auschwitz and Eichmann have rendererd modern man, with all his brilliance and all his arrogance, obsolete.

Man: a divine experiment

Strange that the Hebrew prophets and their successors had no illusions about the nature of man. They did not view him as some ideal being shielded from all temptation, protected by divine fiat from the consequence of his deeds, a semi-angelic creature whose future was secure for all times.

From the beginning the creation of man was a doubtful venture. This is the verdict of more than a few of the ancient sages of Israel.

In the first chapter of Genesis we read: "In the beginning *God* created the heavens and the earth."

In the second chapter of Genesis we read: ". . . the *Lord God* created the heavens and the earth." Why is "God" the

Creator in the first chapter and "the Lord God" in the second chapter?

This was the Rabbinic explanation: There are two Hebrew names for the Divinity: *Elohim,* translated, God; and *Adonoi,* translated, Lord. The Bible uses the name *Elohim* (God) to emphasize the quality of divine *justice,* and *Adonoi* (Lord) to emphasize the quality of divine *mercy.* Thus at first the Divinity planned to create the world on the basis of strict justice. Therefore it is written in the first chapter of Genesis:

> In the beginning God (*Elokim*=divine justice) created the heavens and the earth.

But when He saw the sinful nature of man and realized the world could not survive if it were to be judged solely on the basis of strict justice, He added the quality of mercy and caused it to precede the quality of justice that the world might persist. So it is written in the second chapter of Genesis:

> ". . . The Lord (*Adonoi*=divine mercy) God created the heavens and the earth."

Likewise in the creation of man, in the first chapter of Genesis, we read: "And *God* created man;" while in the second chapter of Genesis, we read: "Then the *Lord God* formed man."

Again, "God" is the creator of man in the first chapter, but it is "the Lord God" in the second chapter. Notice that both in this example and in the one above, divine mercy was not only added but made to *precede* divine justice, as if to tell us: The Almighty wanted to found His world and human society on absolute justice, and even commenced to do so, but He soon perceived that this could not be. Mercy must be joined to justice, indeed, it must precede it, otherwise neither the world nor man can survive. (*Rashi* to Genesis 1.1; cf. *Midrash Yelamdenu.*)

According to a rabbinic parable of creation, (*Breshit Rabbah* 8.) God created and destroyed many worlds before He created ours. When He was about to make man, we are told, great consternation arose in heaven. The forces of truth and justice arose to oppose the creation of man. For if the truth were known and pure justice were exercised, man could never be created, since he could not survive God's justice. Therefore, according to the rabbis, God cast the truth away, put aside justice for mercy and, while the angels were weighing the merits of the case—whether or not man should be created—God created him.

Has man been able to justify God's hope? The Talmud relates that the Schools of Hillel and Shammai disputed two and a half years whether it would have been better if man had or had not been created. Finally they agreed that it would have been better had he not been created, but since he had been created, let him examine his past deeds and take care in what he is about to do. *Eruvin* 13b

What the ancients expressed through biblical exegesis and fanciful fable, we would put differently today. The form of their expression and its strangeness to us disappears, however, when we examine what they were trying to say. The Bible taught them that man exists through God's grace and not by His justice. This is fundamental. For if pure justice were to prevail man would be destroyed. But God tempers His justice with mercy and thus man survives. Man's continued existence is not guaranteed; it is, on the contrary, tenuous and dependent. The angels opposed the creation of man; the forces of truth and justice opposed the creation of man. The creation of man was opposed because the evil that would come forth from him was foreseen. The creation of man was opposed because man's power to hurt, his will to destroy, was foreseen. Notwithstanding, God created man (according to the rabbis) in the hope that the good would conquer the evil, the power to love would conquer the power to hurt, and the will to obey His will would conquer the will to destroy. The history of man, however, has been the history of God's disappointment with man.

Indeed the Bible may be described as God's search for the righteous man, and His repeated disappointment.

Adam disappointed God. His first act was rebellion against God.

> They knew that they were naked. . . . **And** they heard the voice of the Lord God amongst the trees of the

garden. And the Lord God called unto man, and said unto him, "Where art thou?"

Where art thou? God cried. What has happened to this creature I made to rule My earth, to dwell in a garden paradise and to serve Me?

Therefore the Lord God sent him forth from the Garden of Eden, to till the ground from whence he was taken. So He drove out the man.

Communion between God and man had been hampered. Cain disappointed God. He slew his brother, Abel.

And the Lord said unto Cain: "Where is Abel thy brother?" And he said: "I know not; am I my brother's keeper?" And He said, "What hast thou done? The voice of thy brother's blood crieth out unto Me from the ground."

Communion between man and man had been hampered. God called out to both Adam and Cain. Both denied their guilt.

And the Lord saw that the wickedness of man was great in the earth, and that every imagination of the thoughts of his heart was evil continually. And it repented the Lord that He had made on earth, and it grieved Him at His heart. And the Lord said: "I will blot out man whom I have created from the face of the earth; both man and beast, and creeping thing, and fowl of the air; for it repenteth Me that I have made them."

God regretted that He had made man, Scripture tells us, and was about to destroy him, but in His mercy permitted man to begin anew through Noah, who seemed a righteous man. All the rest of mankind was swept away in the flood, and it was as if Noah was again the first man. But Noah, too, disappointed God. He was a drunkard; and his descendants in their rebellious pride built a great tower reaching up to the heavens, so that they might know the divine mysteries and themselves become gods. Again God punished them by confounding their language so that "they would not understand one another's speech," and "scattered them abroad from thence upon the face of all the earth."

Should the human experiment continue? Was it not a failure? Another chance, perhaps his last, was given man. This time God placed His hope in one family and in the people that would come from them: Abraham, Isaac, Jacob, the children of Israel. A small people, crushed by slavery, and therefore open, perhaps, to His word. He revealed His will to this people at Sinai, transforming them into a kingdom of priests and a holy nation, that through them the world might come to know the Lord and follow His ways. If mankind will accept the Torah, the rabbis taught, the world will survive; but if they will not, it will be turned back into chaos.

Adam failed.

Cain failed.

Noah failed.

The generation of the Tower of Babel failed.

Is it so utterly inconceivable that man's last chance was given with the covenant at Sinai?

Is it inconceivable to believe that if Judaism, and Christianity, fail, there will be an end?

Ludicrous as this may have sounded a century ago, it does not sound ludicrous at all today. The "word" has been heard and distorted; the "light" seen and concealed; the "presence" known and avoided. Man has closed the door of his soul to the Source of his being. Perhaps our earth will take its place among the others which God was said to have created and destroyed. Perhaps the time of reckoning has come and God is abandoning us to ourselves.

Some of those who emerged from the raging inferno of human hell in our world which permeated the Nazi death-camps have concluded that man has reached the end of his tether. This seems to be the implicit message in Schwarzbart's classic, *The Last of the Just,* which is based upon the old Jewish legend, going back to the Talmud, that the world is sustained because of the virtue of thirty-six "just men" who live in assumed humble guises in each generation. Schwarzbart's point is that his hero Ernie is the "last of the just";

God's mercy is exhausted, His grace is at an end, His saving power has been withdrawn. A world in which Nazi atrocities could have happened, he tells us, no longer deserves to exist. It is beyond redemption.

When one of the Gemini astronauts was walking out in space, he disobeyed orders to return to the capsule. The official reason given was because he was overcome with excitement at the magnificent view and the novel experience. But one reporter who talked to him at length gave a different reason privately. He said the astronaut disobeyed orders to return, because his deepest self did not want to go back to a cursed planet which had been befouled by Hiroshima and Auschwitz and was about to explode. Something within him rebelled at the thought of living on the earth once again after having come so close to a new start elsewhere.

> Emblazoned over the gates of the world in which we live—writes Abraham Heschel—is the escutcheon of the demons. The mark of Cain in the face of man has come to overshadow the likeness of God. There has never been so much guilt and distress, agony and terror. At no time has the earth been so soaked with blood. Fellow men have turned out to be evil spirits, monstrous and weird. Does not history look like a stage for the dance of might and evil—with man's wits too feeble to separate the two— and God either directing or indifferent to it? The major folly of this view seems to be in its shifting the responsibility for man's plight from man to God, in accusing the Invisible though iniquity is ours. Rather than submit to our own guilt, we seek like Adam, to shift the blame upon someone else. For generations we have been investing life with ugliness and now we wonder why we do not succeed. God was thought of as a watchman hired to prevent us from using our loaded guns. Having failed us, He is now thought of as the ultimate scapegoat.
>
> The roar of the bombers over Rotterdam, Warsaw, London was but the echo of thoughts bred for years by individual brains, and later applauded by entire nations. It was through our failure that people started to suspect that science is a device for exploitation, parliaments

pulpits for hyprocrisy, and religion a pretext for a bad conscience. The conscience of the world was destroyed by those who were wont to blame others rather than themselves. Let us remember. We reversed the instinct but distrusted the prophets. We labored to perfect engines and let our inner life go to wreck. We ridiculed superstition until we lost our ability to believe.

We have helped to extinguish the light our fathers had kindled. We have bartered holiness for convenience, loyalty for success, love for power, wisdom for information, tradition for fashion. In our everyday life we worshipped force, despised compassion and obeyed no law but our unappeasable appetite. The vision of the sacred has all but died in the soul of man. And when greed, envy, and the reckless will to power came to maturity, the serpents cherished in the bosom of our civilization broke out of their dens to fall upon the helpless nations.

We cannot dwell at ease under the sun of our civilization as our ancestors thought we could. What was in the minds of our martyred brothers in their last hours? They died with disdain and scorn for a civilization in which the killing of civilians could become a carnival of fun, for a civilization which gave us mastery over the forces of nature but lost control over the forces of our self.

We live in an age when most of us have ceased to be shocked by the increasing breakdown in moral inhibitions. . . . The decay of conscience fills the air with a pungent smell. Good and evil, which were once as distinguishable as day and night, have become a blurred mist. God is not silent. He has been silenced. We have witnessed in history how often a man, a group or a nation lost sight of God, acts and succeeds, strives and achieves, but is given up by Him. God has withdrawn from their life, even while they are heaping wickedness upon cruelty and malice upon evil. The dismissal of man, the abrogation of Providence, inaugurates eventual calamity. We are left alone, neither molested by punishment, nor assured by indication of help. The divine does not interfere with our actions nor intervene in our conscience. Having all in abundance save His blessing, we find our wealth a shell in which there is curse without mercy.

We have trifled with the name of God. We have called for the Lord. He came. And He was ignored. We have preached but eluded Him. We have praised but defied Him. Now we reap the fruits of our failure. Through centuries His voice cried in the wilderness. How skillfully it was trapped and imprisoned in our temples! How often it was drowned or distorted! Now we behold how it gradually withdraws, abandoning one people after another, departing from their souls, despising their wisdom. The taste for the good has all but gone from earth. Men heap spite upon cruelty, malice upon atrocity. Silence hovers mercilessly over many dreadful lands. The day of the Lord is a day without the Lord. Like Moses, we hide our face; for we are afraid to look upon *Elokim,* upon His power of judgment.

See! the Lord's hand is not too short to save,
Nor His ear too dull to hear;
But your iniquities have been a barrier
Between you and your God.
And your sins have hidden His face
So that He could not hear you.
For your hands are stained with blood,
And your fingers with iniquity:
Your lips have spoken lies,
And your tongue utters untruths.
There is none who sues honestly,
None who pleads his case truthfully.
But each one trusts in vanity and speaks lies,
Conceives wrong, and brings forth mischief.

Therefore is justice far from us,
And righteousness does not reach us;
We look for light, but lo! darkness,
For rays of dawn, but we walk in gloom.
We grope like blind men along a wall,
Like men without eyes we grope;
We stumble at noonday as in the twilight,
In the strength of manhood we are like the dead.

We growl like bears,
And moan like doves;
We look for redress, but it comes not,
For salvation, but it remains far from us.

(*Isaiah* 50:1-11)

What the prophets feared most was God's abandon-
ment of man, the silencing of His voice, the withdrawal
of His presence.
Perhaps this is the deepest meaning of our time.
If man wants to destroy himself,
God seems to say,
Let him.
I have had enough.
I shall try again elsewhere.
There is no guarantee that God will intervene to save
our world from disaster.

A MODERN PARABLE

6

A Modern Parable

I N A WORLD such as ours which brings men, trembling with disbelief, to the brink of finality, to that total sealing off from all that was, is, or might be, would we not expect an outcry so loud the mountains would quake, a weeping so vast the oceans would fill with tears? Where is that outcry and where the tears? Where is the clamoring for a new world and where the prayers? Where is the utter change of heart and where the shame? Where are the great minds of our time to lead us, and where the great books they are writing to guide us? Why is it that most thinkers are *not* thinking about this concern, and most writers are *not* writing about this concern, but rather of other concerns, their own perhaps, concerns in any case which will be no one's concern unless "the" concern is solved.

A strange phenomenon is taking place: fantasy and truth have exchanged places. Some of the writers who have spun tales out of the present debacle have created stories whose fantasy, strangely enough, appears truer than the complacent world in which we live from day to day. It is as if we were living in two worlds: one the world of business, eating, playing, ordinary affairs; the other the world of incredible and apparently inevitable horror about to tear us to pieces. Like some massive schizophrenia in which the normal reaction to danger is stifled by the drawing of an imaginary line, not only in our minds but in our lives, between what we know to be true and what we refuse to take seriously—we persist in dwelling in a dream world of creature-comfort security, transforming reality into fantasy.

Almost all of the creative works dealing with the nuclear threat are pessimistic, while our everyday world is so optimistic. These books reflect mounting despair, while we are excited by the latest home run contest. These books are sombre in tone, while we are still in search of amusement on the movie and TV screens. We assume that some mythical "they" will attend to the mess we find ourselves in as easily as one changes the baby's diaper. The stories whose subject is atomic war contain variables of place, time, and situation, but the essential content of these stories is again and again the same—destruction. It might be well to cite some excerpts from one such work, since the artist often goes beyond the limiting categories of the thinker in plumbing the depths of an idea. And when one reads these tales contrived out of human imagination, the causes are so plausible, the events so realistic, the conclusions so believable, that one would hardly be surprised if fiction were to become fact.

"There won't be anyone around to write a book about World War III after it's over," wrote H. Wheeler, author of *Failsafe*. "That's why we wrote it now. We've reached a point in history where the crisis is so grave and the issues so imponderable that only a forceful novel can teach the lessons of political theory."

Let this tale of eerie science fiction, which is in reality, neither eerie nor fiction but a prose poem parable of profound meaning, act as the bridge between the analysis in the preceding pages and the solution which will be presented in the pages to come—a summary better than any I could summon of what may loom upon the horizon of mankind.

In *A Canticle for Liebowitz* by Walter A. Miller, the symbol of the remote abbeys of the dark ages, in whose cloistered chambers the light of learning flickered waiting to be taken up again with the dawn of the Rennaisance, is updated a thousand years to serve that same purpose once again in the utter midnight which follows upon and continues long after the nuclear war which obliterates the bodies and minds of most of mankind. The "flame deluge" is described in one of the manuscripts hidden in the Abbey of Liebowitz.

Now even as in the time of Job, when the sons of God came to stand before the Lord, Satan also was present among them.

And the Lord said to him: 'Whence comest thou, Satan?'

And Satan answering said, as of old: 'I have gone roundabout the earth, and have walked through it.'

And the Lord said to him: 'Hast thou considered that simple and upright prince, my servant Name, hating evil and loving peace?'

And Satan answering said: 'Doth Name fear God in vain? For hast Thou not blessed his land with great wealth and made him mighty among nations? But stretch forth Thy hand a little and decrease what he hath, and let his enemy be strengthened, then see if he blasphemeth Thee not to Thy face.'

And the Lord said to Satan: 'Behold what he hath, and lessen it. See thou to it.'

And Satan went forth from the presence of God and returned into the world.

Now the Prince Name was not as Holy Job, for when his land was afflicted with trouble and his people less rich than before, when he saw his enemy become mightier, he grew fearful and ceased to trust in God, thinking unto himself: I must strike before the enemy overwhelmeth me without taking his sword in hand.

And so it was in those days that the princes of Earth had hardened their hearts against the Law of the Lord, and of their pride there was no end. And each of them thought within himself that it was better for all to be destroyed than for the will of other princes to prevail over his. For the mighty of the Earth did contend among themselves for supreme power overall; by stealth, treachery, and deceit they did seek to rule, and of war they feared greatly and did tremble; for the Lord God had suffered the wise men of those times to learn the means by which the world itself might be destroyed, and into their hands was given the sword of the Archangel wherewith Lucifer had been cast down, that men and princes might fear God and humble themselves before the Most High. But they were not humbled.

And Satan spoke unto a certain prince, saying Fear not to use the sword, for the wise men have deceived you in saying that the world would be destroyed thereby. . . Strike, and know that you shall be king over all.

And the prince did heed the word of Satan, and he summoned all of the wise men of that realm and called upon them to give him counsel as to the ways in which the enemy might be destroyed without bringing down the wrath upon his own kingdom. But most of the wise men said, 'Lord, it is not possible, for your enemies also have the sword which we have given you.' . . . and the fieriness of it as the flame of Hell and as the fury of the sun-star from whence it was kindled.

Then thou shalt make me yet another which is yet seven times hotter than Hell itself, commanded the prince, whose arrogance had come to surpass that of Pharaoh.

And many of them said: 'Nay, Lord, ask not this thing of us; for even the smoke of such a fire, if we were to kindle it for thee, would cause many to perish.'

Now the prince was angry because of their answer, and he suspected them of betraying him, and he sent his spies among them to tempt them and to challenge them; whereupon the wise men became afraid. Some among them changed their answers, that his wrath be not invoked against them. Three times he asked them, and three times they answered; 'Nay, Lord, even your own people will perish if you do this thing.' But one of the magi . . . having betrayed his brothers, lied to all the people, advising them not to fear the demon Fallout. The prince heeded this false wise man, whose name was Blackeneth, and he caused spies to accuse many of the magi before the people.

Being afraid, the less wise among the magi counseled the prince according to his pleasure, saying: 'The weapons may be used, only to not exceed such-and-such a limit, or all will surely perish.'

And the prince smote the cities of his enemies with the new fire, and for three days and nights did his great catapults and metal birds rain wrath upon them. Over each city a sun appeared and was brighter than the sun of heaven, and immediately that city withered and melted as wax under the streets and their skins smoked and they became fagots thrown on the coals. And when the fury of the sun had faded, the city was in flames; and a great thunder came out of the sky, like great battering-ram PIK-A-DON, to crush it utterly. Poisonous fumes fell over all the land, and the land was aglow by night with the afterfire and the curse of the afterfire which caused a scurf on the skin and made the hair to fall and the blood to die in the veins.

And a great stink went up from Earth even unto Heaven. Like unto Sodom and Gomorrah was the Earth and the ruins thereof, even in the land of that certain prince, for his enemies did not withhold their vengeance, sending fire in turn to engulf his cities as their own. The stink of the carnage was exceedingly offensive to the Lord, Who spoke unto the prince, Name, saying.

WHAT BURNT OFFERING IS THIS THAT YOU HAVE PRE-PARED BEFORE ME? WHAT IS THIS SAVOR THAT ARISES FROM THE PLACE OF HOLOCAUST? HAVE YOU MADE ME A HOLO-CAUST OF SHEEP OR GOATS, OR OFFERED A CALF UNTO GOD?

But the prince answered him not, and God said: YOU HAVE MADE ME A HOLOCAUST OF MY SONS.

And the Lord slew him together with **Blackeneth**, the betrayer, and there was pestilence in the **Earth, and** madness was upon mankind, who stoned the wise together with the powerful, those who remained.

One Abbey, the Abbey of Saint Liebowitz, seeks to preserve in its memorabilia the few remaining books of mankind for a future society that may once more reconstruct a new civilization upon the ashes and ruins of the old. This is how it came about:

> Within weeks—some said days—it was ended, after the first unleashing of the hell fire. Cities had become puddles of glass, surrounded by vast acreages of broken stone. While nations had vanished from the earth, the lands littered with bodies, both men and cattle, and all the manner of beasts, together with the birds of the air and all things that flew, all things that swam in the rivers, crept in the grass, or burrowed in holes; having sickened and perished, they covered the land, and yet where the demons of the Fallout covered the country side, the bodies for a time would not decay, except in contact with fertile earth. The great clouds of wrath engulfed the forests and the fields, withering trees and causing the crops to die. There were great deserts where once life was and in those places of the Earth where men still lived, all were sickened by the poisoned air, so that, while some escaped death, none was left untouched; and many died even in those lands where the weapons had not struck, because of the poisoned air.
>
> In all parts of the world men fled from one place to other places, and there was confusion of tongues. Much wrath was kindled against the princes and the servants of the princes and against the magi who had devised the weapons. Years passed, and yet the Earth was not cleaned. So it was clearly recorded in the Memorabilia.
>
> From the confusion of tongues, the intermingling of the remnants of many nations, from fear, the hate was born. And the hate said: *Let us stone and disembowel and burn the ones who did this thing. Let us make a holocaust of those who wrought this crime, together with their hirelings and their names, and even their memories. Let us destroy them all, and teach our children that the world is new, that they may know nothing of the deeds that went before. Let us make a great simplification, and then the world shall begin again.*
>
> So it was that, after the Deluge, the Fallout, the plagues, madness, the confusion of tongues, the rage, there be-

gan the blood-letting of the Simplification, when remnants of mankind had torn other remnants limb from limb, killing rulers, scientists, leaders, technicians, teachers, and whatever persons the leaders of the maddened mobs said deserved death for having helped to make the Earth what it had become. Nothing had been so hateful in the sight of these mobs as the man of learning, at first because they had served the princes, but then later because they refused to join in the bloodletting and tried to oppose the mobs, calling the crowds "bloodthirsty simpletons."

Joyfully the mobs accepted the name, took up the cry: *Simpletons! yes, yes! I'm a simpleton! Are you a simpleton? We'll build a town and we'll name it Simple Town, because by then all the smart bastards that caused all this, they'll be dead! Simpletons! Lets go! This ought to show 'em! Anybody here not a simpleton? Get the bastard, if there is!*

The simplification had ceased to have plan or purpose soon after it began, and became an insane frenzy of mass murder and destruction such as can occur only when the last traces of social order are gone. The madness was transmitted to the children, taught as they were—not merely to forget—but to hate, and surges of mob fury recurred sporadically even through the fourth generation after the Deluge. By then, the fury was directed not against the learned, for there were none, but against the merely literate.

Isaac Edward Leibowitz, after a fruitless search for his wife, had fled to the Cistercians where he remained in hiding during the early post-Deluge years. He gathered a few companions about him and made some quiet proposals. . . . Twelve years after the proposals were made, Father Isaac Edward Leibowitz had won permission from the Holy See to found a new community. . . . Its task, unannounced, and at first only vaguely defined, was to preserve human history for the great-great-great-grandchildren of the children of the simpletons who wanted it destroyed. Its earliest habit was burlap rags and bindlestiffs—the uniform of the simpleton mob. Its members were either 'bookleggers' or 'memorizers,' according to the tasks assigned. The bookleggers smuggled books to the southwest desert and buried them there in kegs. The memorizers committed to rote memory entire volumes of history, sacred writings, literature, and science, in case some unfortunate book smuggler was caught, tortured, and forced to reveal the location of the kegs. Meanwhile, other members of the New Order located a water hole about three days' journey from the book cache and began the building of a monastery. The project, aimed at saving a small remnant of human culture from the remnant of humanity who wanted it destroyed, was then underway.

The memorizers were few, their memories limited.

Some of the book kegs were found and burned, as well as several other bookleggers. The monastery itself was attacked thrice before the madness subsided.

From the vast store of human knowledge, only a few kegs of original books and a pitiful collection of hand-copied texts, rewritten from memory, had survived in the possession of the Order by the time the madness had ended.

Now, after six centuries of darkness, the monks still preserved this Memorabilia, studied it, copied and re-copied it, and patiently waited. At the beginning, in the time of Leibowitz, it had hoped—and even anticipated as probable—that the fourth or fifth generation would begin to want its heritage back. But the monks of the earliest days had not counted on the human ability to generate a new cultural inheritance in a couple of generations if an old one is utterly destroyed, to generate it by virtue of lawgivers and prophets, geniuses or maniacs; through a Moses, or through a Hitler, or an ignorant but tyrannical grandfather, a cultural inheritance may be acquired between dusk and dawn, and many have been so acquired. But the new 'culture' was an inheritance of darkness, wherein 'simpleton' meant the same thing as 'citizen' meant the same thing as slave. The monks waited. It mattered not at all to them that the knowledge they saved was useless, that much of it was not really knowledge now, was as inscrutable to the monks in some instances as it would be to an illiterate wild-boy from the hills; this knowledge was empty of content, its subject matter long since gone.

Haunting the Abbey of Liebowitz for millennia is an old wanderer, Benjamin by name, a Jew, mysterious in his ways and always dwelling apart. He waits, ever waits, never dies but waits for the coming of Him whose hope he carries. He knows that the One for whom he waits is somewhere present in every generation, if only he could find Him. But Benjamin does not find the anointed for whom he is waiting. Meanwhile, centuries pass and once again man crawls forward into the world of understanding. Once again science advances, putting one block atop another, building generation upon generation, until at last what the twentieth century knew is known a second time, the Memorabilia of the Abbey of Saint Leibowitz is comprehended; skyscrapers are erected, planes search the air, submarines explore the sea—and atomic power returns! With its return the nations arm a second time and the world is threatened with a second flame deluge.

Brothers—said the abbot, approaching the lectern— let us not assume that there is going to be war. Let's remind ourselves that Lucifer has been with us—this time—for nearly two centuries. And it was dropped only twice, in sizes smaller than megaton. We all know what could happen, if there's war. The genetic festering is still with us from the last time Man tried to eradicate himself. Back then, in the Saint Leibowitz' time, maybe they didn't know what would happen. Or perhaps they did know, but could not quite believe it until they tried it—like a child who knows what a loaded pistol is supposed to do, but who never pulled a trigger before. They had not yet seen a billion corpses. They had not seen the madness and the murder and the blotting out of reason. Then they did it, and then they saw it.

Now—now the princes, the presidents, the praesidiums, now they know—with dead certainty. They can know it by the children they beget and send to asylums for the deformed. They know it, and they've kept the peace. Not Christ's peace, certainly, but peace, until lately— with only two warlike incidents in as many centuries. Now they have the bitter certainty. My sons, they cannot do it again. Only a race of madmen could do it again.

But a race of madmen it is; war is declared, and the fire deluge has again begun to fall upon earth. One small ship carrying the Memorabilia, some priests and others are to be sent to another planet to begin life anew.

Someone had opened the abbey doors. Monks were leaving quietly for their cells. Only a dim glow spilled from the doorway into the courtyard. The light was dim in the church. Joshua could see only a few candles and the dim red eye of the sanctuary lamp. The twenty-six of his brethren were just visible where they knelt, waiting. Someone closed the doors again, but not quite for through a crack he could still see the red dot of the sanctuary lamp. Fire kindled in worship, burning gently in adoration there in its red receptacle. Fire, loveliest of the four elements of the world, and yet an element too in Hell. While it burned adoringly in the core of the Temple, it had also scorched the life from a city this night, and spewed its venom over the land. How strange of God to speak from a burning bush, and of Man to make a symbol of Heaven into a symbol of Hell. . . .

They were but a handful, these celestial colonists of *Homo loquaz nonnumquam sapiens,* a few harassed colonies of humanity that had had small help from Earth thus far; and now they might expect no help at all, there in their new non-Edens, even less like Paradise than Earth had been. Fortunately for them, perhaps. The closer men came to perfecting for themselve a paradise, the more impatient they seemed to become with it, and with themselves as well. They made a garden of pleasure, and became progressively more miserable with it as it grew in richness and power and beauty; for then, perhaps, it was easier for them to see that something was missing in the garden, some tree or shrub that would not grow. When the world was in darkness and wretchedness, it could believe in perfection and yearn for it. . . . Well, they were going to destroy it again, were they—this garden Earth, civilized and knowing, to be torn apart again that Man might hope again in wretched darkness.

And yet the Memorabilia was to go with the ship! Was it a curse? *Discede, Seductor informis!* It was no curse, this knowledge, unless perverted by Man, as fire had been, this night. . . .

Destiny always seems decades away, but suddenly it's not decades away; it's right now. But maybe destiny is always right now, right here, right this very instant, maybe.

Abbot Zerchi boarded the plane briefly before take-off—for last farewells:

You are the continuity of the Order, he told them. "With you goes the Memorabilia. You will be years in space. The ship will be your monastery . . . . If civilization, or a vestige of it, can maintain itself, you will send missions to the other colony worlds, and perhaps eventually to the colonies of their colonies. Wherever Man goes, you and your successors will go. And with you, the records and remembrances of four thousand years and more. Some of you, or those to come after you, will be mendicants and wanderers, teaching the chronicles of Earth . . . to the peoples and the culture that may grow out of the colony groups. For some may forget. Be for Man the memory of Earth and Origin. Remember this Earth. Never forget her, but—never come back . . . . If you ever come back, you might meet the Archangel at the east end of the Earth, guarding her passes with a sword of flame. I feel it. Space is your home hereafter. It's lonelier desert than ours. God bless you, and pray for us. . . .

He watched until the plane disappeared from view in the evening sky. Afterward, he drove back to the abbey and to the remainder of his flock. While aboad the plane, he had spoken as if the destiny of Brother Joshua's group were as clear-cut as the prayers prescribed for tomorrow's Office; but both he and they knew that he had only been reading the palm of a plan, had been describing a hope and not a certainty. For Brother Joshua's group had only begun the first short lap of a long and doubtful journey, a new Exodus from Egypt under the auspices of a God who must surely be very weary of the race of Man. Those who stayed behind had the easier part. Theirs was but to wait for the end and pray that it would not come.

A RADICAL SOLUTION
TO A RADICAL SITUATION

When a child wants to know about war, what does
a parent say that is honest, clear and meaningful?
How can we avoid either deception on the one hand,
or a distressing confession of our immaturity on the
other? . . . The next war could easily exterminate
mankind. Children today feel that the adult world
has not solved the problem of living together—only
of dying together.
          —Sidney J. Harris, *Chicago Daily News*

Take him aside and tell him Yes, we are in it together:
The rich with their automatic comforts, and the family
    bunking seven in a room:
The trained, who understand poems and cybernetics, and
    the boys in leather jackets who browse through comic
    books at the corner newsstand:
Old people tired of wars and winters, and children who
    do not yet know they are made of matter:
The famous face in four colors, nationalized on the cover
    of the magazine; and the crowd face, the background
    face, gray, nameless, out of focus:
We are in it together.

Tell him the secrets of the earth have been peeled, one
    by one, until the core is bare:
The recipes are private, in guarded codes, but the stink
    of death is public, as always when orders come down
    for the big kill.
Tell him no covenant is so openly arrived at as that be-
    tween the murderable masses and their murderers.
Tell him there have been improvements since the good
    old days of Nagasaki; that the atom can be more sullen
    than has yet been shown:

. . . Tell him we are all in the zone of danger: in it
    together: Seat Belt Fastened:
Tell him what has become of the victors and their vic-
    tories
And how those who spoiled for war were spoiled for
    peace:

Tell him how epochs hang on the tailored charms of diplomats:

Tell him how we should have learned by now that every multiple of one comes to but One in the arithmetic of nations:

That unless we work at it together, at a single earth,

There will be others out of the just-born and the not-yet contracted for, who will die for our invisible daily mistakes. . . .

But tell him also that alarm is easier than pride to point with:

We are in it together, and that, when held up to a certain light, is good as much as ill:

For Oneness is our destination, has long been: is by far the best of places to arrive at:

The chemicking that could destroy us can also do as bidden by us: outmaneuver genii; be servile to the meek; reform our wayward systems peacefully.

Tell him the choice rests in the care of what fragile peace we have: including his trusteeship, if he but live to his majority:

One, or nothing: wealth, or laying waste:

Men, or Jew and Gentile: men, or the color of men:

These are the choices, and we make them daily.

Tell him he must learn to answer for himself.

                —Norman Corwin, *Overkill and Megalove*

It is war . . .

I say the word—it has no meaning.

How can they truly be at war?

I remember when we first turned the key of formula

And mocked the Sun,

Some of the architects of fission

Built a clock,

And set it ticking

And said for all to hear:

"We have moved the clock of science a hundred years ahead of time.

That ticking is a time bomb of extinction

Unless you quickly move equal years ahead
Within your own hearts."

—The Night of the Auk

Men must choose to be governed by God or they con-
demn themselves to be ruled by tyrants.

—William Penn

The sun rises when morning comes;
The mist rises from the meadow;
The dew rises from the clover;
But oh, when will my heart arise?

—Welsh song

And then all her former fear falls away, and she knows
clearly she is free, and sings with joy to see herself in
such serene and tranquil peace.

—John of the Cross

7

A Radical Solution
to a Radical Situation

Nㅇㄴㅌ OF THE THREE suggested solutions—military defense, international agreement nor God's miraculous intervention—is the solution we are seeking. But this does not mean that there is no solution. There is. Indeed we enter into it from the conclusion of our discussion of the role of God in the life of man.

There is a solution to the problem of nuclear war and the possible end of human life.. But it is a radical solution. It must be so. It can only be so. A radical situation demands a radical solution. Nothing short of that will avail.

"Radical" comes from the Latin and means "going to the root." It is there, in the roots of the human enterprise, rather than in economic reform or a master plan for world government, that the ultimate answer lies: in that depth which, on the one hand, reaches beyond all partial proposals and, on the other hand, is their foundation, the only real hope for their fulfillment.

The blessing or the curse

Perhaps the clearest expression of our solution is found in this passage of the Bible:

> *I call heaven and earth to witness against you this day,*
> *that I have set before thee life and death,*
> *the blessing and the curse;*
> *therefore choose life, that thou mayest live, thou and thy*
>   *seed;*
> *to love thy Lord thy God*
> *to hearken to His voice,*
> *and to cleave unto Him:*
> *for that is thy life and the length of thy days . . .*
> *If you obey the commandment of the Lord thy God*
> *which I command you this day*
> *by loving the Lord thy God,*
> *by walking in His ways,*
> *and by keeping His commandments . . .*
> *then you shall live*
> *and multiply*
> *and the Lord thy God will bless you. . .*
> *But if your heart turns away and you will not hear,*
> *but are drawn away to worship other gods and serve them,*
> *I declare unto you this day,*
> *that you shall surely perish. . . .*
>
> (Deut. 30:19, 20; 15-18)

These ancient words, hoary with time and memory, were written down in an ancient book by an ancient people who claimed that they had been confronted by God, and had learned the truth about man for all time—that he is dust and image and finite freedom.

These simple yet profound Biblical words contain the answer we seek. What do they say?

That man, who is both grandeur and misery, image and dust, is placed on earth with freedom of will to choose: the evil way or the good way, the blessing or the curse.

That God urges us to choose the good way, to love the Lord and walk in His ways. For in that way lies life, length of days and blessing.

But that there is always the other way, and it is a tempting way: the worship of false gods as the true God, the idols of nature, society and the ego, of man himself. In that way lies the curse and death, for the idol becomes a demon which ultimately destroys those who worship it.

Moses has been right all these years, but the truth of his words has been ignored by the majority of mankind. It seemed perfectly possible in all the ages gone by to swindle, to cheat, to fight, to wage war, to break treaties, to seek power, to deny every law of God and man—and still get along, even to flourish. By and large, in the past, the man who loved God and obeyed His law was rewarded with a joyous life, and, by and large, those who violated God's law inherited misery. But that was only "by and large," and even the lesson of "by and large" did not convince everyone, because it seemed easier and more tempting to be one's own god, live for one's own interests, and serve one's own welfare. There were also history's Jobs to consider, those whose innocence did not prevent the wrath of sickness, poverty, and anguish from reaching them; and the kings and princes and merchants and generals and pirates and gangsters and criminals of all ages to consider, those whose evil deeds, far from bringing them misery, rewarded them with untold wealth, power, and pleasure.

Thus, warfare, bloody as it might have been, never deterred future wars, because it was not a matter of life and death for the universe.

Crime, harmful as it might have been, never deterred future tyrants, because it was not a matter of life and death for the universe.

Cruelty, corruption, depravity, and the horrors which resulted from them throughout the course of history, never prevented their regular reoccurrence, because it was not a matter of life and death for the universe.

The world, in the past, has been able to tolerate vast amounts of evil and still maintain itself. But today it has reached the saturation point.

This is the unending chasm that divides all that has gone before us from that which lies ahead.

In the past, loving God, walking in His way, and obeying His commandments was looked upon as desirable, the proper thing to do. Some even took it seriously and devoted their lives to His service; many more took it half-heartedly, but at least allowed it to play some role in their lives. Still, if there were people who did not walk in God's ways—who defiled, corrupted and oppressed—the world would survive.

Today it is quite a different matter. Whether or not men walk in God's ways—whether or not men are criminals or responsible citizens, tyrants or dedicated leaders, corrupt or decent, depraved or exalted—is literally *a matter of life and death, of the very survival of the world.* Either there will be a change in man's heart or there will be no man nor heart to change!

Quite a different situation.

A radically different situation.

Requiring a radically different solution.

It almost seems as if the pre-modern concept of divine reward and punishment for human deeds, one of the strongest forces in days gone by to encourage good deeds and prevent evil ones, has again become reinstated. The fiery threat of Hell which motivated so much of the lives of our ancestors, now, ironically, takes on a new form.

There are two differences, however. In the past the fear of punishment was largely relegated to a future world and, in the opinion of scoffers, was nothing but superstition. Today, fear of physical punishment for man's deeds is

(1) moved ahead to our own world, and is

(2) a fear that far from being felt by religious fanatics, is a demonstrated fact in the minds of Nobel-prize winning physicists.

Nevertheless, I am not arguing that men should love **God** and obey His commandments out of fear of punishment alone. This would return us to the argument previously considered of preventing war by mutual fear of retaliation. **Rather it** must awaken us to the terrible relevancy of man's inner life to our outer situation.

Indeed nothing—*nothing*—is more relevant to the problem we face than the condition of the human spirit.

Upsetting the balance

There was once a town in the heart of America where all life seemed to be in harmony with its surroundings. It had fertile farms, prosperous farmers, birds in the trees, fish in the streams, and flowers blooming gaily along the roadside. Then a white powder fell from the sky like snow and a fearful blight crept over the land. Cattle and sheep sickened. Hens could not hatch eggs. Strange illnesses appeared among people. Children were stricken at play and died within a few hours and roadsides were lined with browned vegetation, as if swept by fire.

Such is the picture drawn of the future by Rachel Carson, that gentle lady-scientist who led us into the depths of the ocean's mysteries with two beautiful books some years ago, in her slashing, smashing attack on the three hundred million dollar a year pesticide industry entitled *Silent Spring*. Her thesis, carefully documented and cogently argued, is that the indiscriminate use of insecticides such as DDT threatens to let loose upon man and the countryside a flood of dangerous chemicals which may in time, and has already to some extent, upset the natural harmony throughout nature and threatens calamity for us. She called her book *Silent Spring* because:

> we spray our elms and the following springs are silent of robin song, not because we sprayed the robins directly but because the poison traveled, step by step, through the now familiar elm-leaf-earthworm-robin cycle. We poison the caddis flies in a stream and the salmon runs dwindle and die. We poison the gnats in a lake and the poison travels from link to link of the food chain and soon the birds of the lake margins become its victims. These are matters of record, observable, part of the visible world around us. They reflect the web of life—or death—that scientists know as ecology.

All this is the fault of human carelessness, greed and irresponsibility. In other words, there is a certain balance of forces within nature which enables life to continue. If man comes along in his brusque, brutish way and dares to "upset the balance," then he must beware of the consequences. This, I think, is what Miss Carson is saying to her readers.

Now if there is danger in "upsetting the balance" in the world of nature, what about the world of man? If the natural realm can tolerate only so much foreign substance, what about the human realm? In scanning the pages of history, we learn that spiritually man has been able to contend with the evils of moral waste much as the kidneys rid the body of physical waste. Enormous as infamy may have appeared in the past, man has always possessed sufficient resources to emerge from darkness into light, to rise up from defeat after defeat and struggle onward. But there comes a time when the intake of alcohol, for example, rises beyond the capacity point for the kidneys to function, when huge amounts of insecticides overpower the vast cleansing functions of nature, when man's malevolence grows so enormous as to render inoperable the spiritual dynamics of former ages. So what we always knew could happen within the body of a single man—that his protective resources might under certain circumstances no longer be able to maintain life—and now know can happen for parts of nature—we are compelled to admit is possible for the entire world.

The prophets warned that man cannot lay sin upon sin without consequence—that there might come a time when the amount of evil man does becomes so monstrous that it can be borne no more. This is the judgment which threatens when the toleration point for evil has been reached. Then not only the birds will be silenced, but man himself.

This is precisely the situation we face. The toleration point of evil in history *has* been reached. We are now on the verge of "upsetting the balance" of man himself and, because of man, not just a few million acres, but all creation, all of nature as well. For greater damage will be done to those robins and salmon by nuclear radiation and heat than by any other method. We dare not continue to pollute the stream of human life.

Thus, Miss Carson's book should be read with colored glasses. For "nature," read "history"; for "insecticide" read "radiation." But when she writes about upsetting the balance, she means what we mean: that the toleration point has been reached, that the whistles are shrieking, that the very nature of man is at stake, that you cannot go much further down the road of carelessness and greed without endangering the entire process, that history can bear only so much and no more, that man has been transformed into a frightened spider about to be drenched with that white powder floating down from on high, that the harmony between man and God, and man and man, and man and himself has been fearfully torn asunder, that the balance has been upset, and that if it is not set right, both man and nature will be gone.

It is not as if, down through the ages, man had not endeavored to solve the problems of our world. Man's error was repeated over and over again in a thousand different forms but in essence it was the same error. It was the error of turning relative truths into absolutes. And each time this happened something fallible and finite, the product of man's mind and hands, was raised to the throne of God himself and worshipped as God, as absolute. But when a relative good is turned into an absolute, it becomes a demon that carries us away with it.

The king possesses a divine right; education will do away with evil; *vox populi vox dei;* intelligence can answer all problems; industrialization will end poverty forever; private property is the only way; the state is the perfect society; liberty is all man needs; socialism is the only means to true equality; democracy is the solution to all dilemmas.

These slogans represent some of the false gods of history. They are all partial goods, relative goods—but not absolutes.

The king may claim power above the law and become a tyrant; it depends upon who is king and what his powers are.

The people can turn into a wild mob; it depends upon what motivates the people.

Industrialization and private property can lead to exploitation; it depends upon how they are used.

Education and intelligence can destroy; it depends upon what is made of them.

Science can produce weapons to annihilate mankind; it depends upon how science is utilized.

Democracy by democratic processes can choose to end democracy.

There is nothing inherently wrong with any of the above answers. They are all partial goods, depending on what use is made of them, to what purpose they are put. At certain times, in certain places, under certain conditions, they are good. At other times, in other places, under other circumstances, they are bad. They are bad when man becomes so impressed with their achievement or capacity, that he raises them to the level of absolute good, and they turn into the highest standard by which all else is judged. Such idolatry inevitably leads to disaster. For when a man takes something which he has made and worships it as an idol, setting it upon the very throne of God, it becomes a demon and destroys those who believe in it.

There is only one way to remember that everything human is dependent or relative, and that is by accepting the Lord of justice and mercy, the Creator of heaven and earth, as our God and our absolute. Then there can be no other gods and all else is constantly judged in terms of the one absolute.

The Bible is not against any of the above per se; it only says that they are not enough. Alone these answers can become gods that turn into devils. What gives all of these answers meaning and usefulness is the simple command of the Bible to love God and walk in His ways. We can exist without skyscrapers and air-conditioning, without gas-chambers and H-bombs. But we cannot exist without the spiritual source of our being. The problem is not how to escape civilization—that is impossible—but how to surpass it.

It is not enough to say, not precise enough to say—as is said again and again—that our spiritual progress has not kept up with our technological progress. It is, rather, that *our technological advance has finally reached such a point of absolute power that virtual spiritual perfection is demanded to harness it to good purposes and prevent its being used for evil purposes.*

Dreadful though this prospect is, it defines our position.

Scientific progress has brought us to the spiritual saturation point.

And we are not ready.

The Bible

In this context, a strange thing happens. The Bible becomes what it always has been—the most relevant of all books. The words of Scripture apply today as they did when they were uttered, but only now have they achieved the seriousness of reality. The ancient prophets speaking to you and me. If we really want to understand what is going on in our world, we should put down our newspapers, for the news they report is not the "real" news. It is only a repetition of something that has happened last week in a slightly different fashion, the superficial goings-on of society. But the real news, the eternal and relevant news, is the word of the Bible:

If man walks in the way of God, he will have peace and blessing.

If man rebels against Him and worships gods of his own—the state, power, the ego—he will have death and the end of the world.

Indeed, the validity of this proposition is becoming so apparent today that it would not be surprising if newspapers began carrying it as a headline in the near future.

Biblical thinking has become common-sense thinking.

A statement appeared in a national periodical reporting the recovery of the late Senator Richard Neuberger of Oregon from a severe illness. The Senator had been suffering from an almost fatal bout with cancer and was away from his desk for five months. When he returned he made a statement that, after looking death in the face for months, he now was no longer concerned in the usual power struggles of politics; he was only interested in serving his country and his God as best he could. Formerly an acid-tongued debater, he was transformed overnight into one of the most quiet, thoughtful, and considerate members of the Senate.

Something like this is happening to many of us today—to thinkers, writers, scientists, military men, leaders of our government, even to the man in the street—to all those who are looking into the face of ultimate questions.

For the simple fact is that the ultimate questions of the universe are no longer only for the philosopher or the saint.

They have become peculiarly relevant to the day to day life of every one of us and to the future of our world. The truth is, of course, that they have always been relevant to our life and our world. But this relevancy, the relevancy of revering God and walking in His ways—rarely apparent in the course of history—has now assumed a startling significance to millions of minds, and must of necessity become apparent to millions more. It is only a question of time.

Ultimate issues—good and evil, justice and mercy, the love and law of God—are now *necessary* issues.

Ultimate concerns are now *immediate* concerns. They are now, perhaps, for the first time in the history of mankind, seen in a new light and from the most practical vantage point— not just from the mountain retreat, but from the scientist's lecture and the weekly magazine as well.

The inescapable facts of our situation are forcing us to understand with merciless pressure the very meaning of life itself. Thinking about the meaning of life is not something the man on the street could be expected to be concerned with down through the ages, despite the influence of philosophy, poetry, and religion. The man on the street has always been too much taken up with the pleasures of his body, the satisfaction of his ego, or simply making a livelihood and striving to be like everyone else. But now he faces inescapably the possibility of total annihilation through nuclear attack. And he is forced to begin doing something he has managed to avoid for millennia: *think.*

He soon comes to the solemn and frightening conclusion that life is not simply a game without rules, created solely for his pleasure.

He understands that life must be taken *seriously.*

That man's actions have *consequences.*

That man may be *called to account* for his actions by overwhelming disaster.

That man himself is only an experiment.

Man, the Bible seems to say, is nothing more than a possibility in time, a colossal gamble in joining the holy and the profane, heaven and earth, angel and animal, infinite and finite—a *divine experiment.*

Can it be that the earth, fully conquered by man, will cease to be a place where man wants to live?—asks the eminent Christian thinker, Paul Tillich. Is our passionate push into outer space perhaps an unconscious expression of the flight of man from the earth? There are no safe answers to these questions, but they must be raised because they undercut any false feeling of security in the relation of man to the earth. The old insight that man is but a pilgrim on earth is echoed in these questions applicable today not to single men but to mankind . . . . Mankind itself is a pilgrim on earth, and the moment will arrive in which this pilgrimage comes to an end— perhaps in an indefinitely remote period, perhaps in the very near future. Christianity gives no indication of the length of man's history. The early church expected the end every moment; when it did not come and disappointment grasped the Christians, the span was extended. In modern times the span has been stretched to an unlimited extent. . . . In the old story God repented of having created man. This implies that the creation of man was a risk God took; and every risk carries with it the possibility of failure. God himself considered the creation of man a failure, and he tried again; but nothing assures us that it was not a failure once more. . . . The first time, according to the story, nature executed the divine judgment on man; this time man may do it himself.

There is no guarantee that the divine experiment will succeed. No guarantee at all. Man is given free will to choose to live or die. More than that, there is revelation, that record of man's meeting with the Divine from which he learns what is right for him; there is prayer through which man opens himself to the presence and power of God; there is the "urge for good" implanted within him; and lastly there is reason, the intelligence to understand how doing that which is good will bring blessing and life.

But, revelation and reason (plus conscience and prayer) granted, there is no surety that man will follow the good way, the way of blessing and life. For he is free to choose. And this freedom to choose not only leads to blessing, but to curse. That is why it can be a dreadful freedom.

It is freedom for hatred as well as love,
for competition as well as co-operation.
for betrayal as well as honor,
for corruption as well as improvement,
for neglect as well as duty,
for violence as well as law,
for revenge as well as forgiveness,
for filth as well as purity,
for crime as well as innocence,
for slavery as well as equality,
for barbarity as well as benevolence,
for savagery as well as civilization,
for misery as well as grandeur,
for curse as well as blessing,
for death as well as life.

If man turns his face from God, closing his ear to His word and his heart to His presence, and listens only to the voice of the false gods that tempt and try his soul, then his freedom may end in disaster. For man is a divine experiment, with no guarantee of success; and it is precisely this experimental nature of man's existence, which the Bible has always taught, that men everywhere, awakening from the dreams of history, are suddenly becoming aware of.

When the prophecies of Jules Verne came true—submarines that explore the ocean depths and balloons that soar through the air—people were stunned.

When the cartoon world of Buck Rogers seems about to be realized, they are amazed.

When Aldous Huxley's *Brave New World* of the mass man in the totalitarian society is achieved within the author's own lifetime so that he is compelled to publish a sequel, they are impressed.

But the fulfillment of these predictions is insignificant when we consider the fulfillment of the prophecies Biblical. What the prophet ranted and raved about some twenty-five hundred years ago—that the murder of the innocent would bring destruction upon nations, that the persecution of a stranger could lead to catastrophe, that hurting an orphan was a crime of cosmic proportions, that despising the poor could cause the heavens to shake, that lies and robbery and crime might shatter the foundations of the world—was almost always taken by readers to indicate some manner of ecstatic hysteria which was responsible for the cataclysmic conclusions which they drew from such insignificant causes.

After all, how could good or evil affect the natural order? How could doing wrong jeopardize the existence of the world? This was purely fanatic exaggeration brought on by emotional unbalance.

Oh yes, the prophets' words were read, and we agreed quite solemnly that evil was wrong. In reality, however, we thought that those bearded Hebrew prophets were playing Baron Munchausen. It was nothing but a form of grotesque sensationalism. Why be so drastic, so demanding? There is place for concern for evil and good, for following God's way, and all that sort of thing, but there are other concerns in life too. The prophets take things too seriously. They take all the fun out of life!

For despite the claim of the prophets that, ultimately, the world of nature depends upon the world of the spirit, the reverse has been the view most commonly held in the history of man. The laws of nature—such as that of gravitation which asserts that an object will fall in accordance with its weight and the distance of the drop because of gravitational force—are understood to irrevocably inhere within the structure of the world, governing with absolute sovereignty the workings of both the individual body of man within and the vast nebulae without. These laws of nature are the means of understanding and mastering nature which man has sought to unravel and apply with such amazing success in the past few centuries.

But not only are there laws of nature—scientific law—there is likewise moral law. Moral law is imbedded in the fabric, not of nature, as is scientific law, but of the spirit. Both are laws of life.

We live in the dimension of spirit as well as the one of nature. Man is the link between the two, the knot that joins heaven and earth. Good and evil, right and wrong exist, though man's apprehension of these may not be absolute. Just as the violation of a law of nature—such as gravitation—leads to catastrophe, so does violation of the moral law.

It was usually assumed that the moral and the physical laws were separate dimensions, quite independent of one another, or if they were related, it was the law of nature which was central and upon which the moral law depended. Now the claims of the prophet are understood: that ultimately even the physical laws depend upon the moral laws, that if justice and righteousness are violated too long by too many, the very earth upon which we dwell may explode, and that nature depends upon spirit, the visible upon the invisible, science on ethics, civilization upon mercy, nations upon morality, life and death upon moral decision, the scientific law upon the moral law, the existence of man upon his compatibility with God.

> I looked on the earth, and lo, it was waste and void;
> To the heavens, and they had no light.
> I looked on the mountains, and lo, they were quaking,
> All the hills moved to and fro.
> I looked, and lo, there was no man;
> All the birds of the air had fled.
> I looked, and lo, the fruitful land was a desert;
> All its cities were laid in ruins
> Before the Lord, before His fierce anger.
>
> *(Jeremiah 4:25-26)*

Few people understood in the past that loving God and walking in His ways meant life, while following after the idols of our own creation meant death; that the existence of the world depends on goodness and not steel, on justice and not iron, on mercy and not power.

The world rests upon three pillars, say the ancient Jewish sages: upon God's word, upon man's prayer, and upon his good deeds. It seems to be a foolish statement—the Bible, prayer, and good deeds. The scientist would no doubt claim that the world stands upon natural law, the philosopher upon reason, the tyrant upon power, the business man upon profit. But these are not the real foundations of the world; they cannot guarantee the stability and permanence of our society. They are weak, fallible, and deceitful.

We are now suddenly awakened to the supreme fact: the true foundations of the world are the foundations of the human spirit.

Israel

I have said that few people in the past have understood this. One of those few, in part and from time to time, was the people of Israel. It is not that they were superior to other peoples, but that—whether they willed it or not—their fate was different from others. The Talmud relates that the Lord offered the Torah to many nations but they all rejected it because of the wearisome demands it contained—justice, truth, mercy. Even when it was offered to Israel, they too feared to take it. God, the ancient legend asserts, had to lift Mount Sinai over their heads and proclaim: Either you receive My Torah, or I shall crush you beneath this mountain! The legend implies that Israel stood in awe before its task. And so they had reason to. But they became God's people and His Book became their Book.

A fearsome fate, a fearsome Book.

Many times they rebelled against it and against Him, but they were bound to Him and to their destiny as His messengers unto the world, with unbreakable bonds. The word of God broke out of the hearts of Israel's prophets, and the rabbis forged a discipline of the spirit which enslaved the people once again—not to Pharoah but to the living God.

To live with the Lord, and with the Book, was their destiny. They understood its meaning. They beheld the evil which lurked in the hearts of men; they knew that the world was in exile, unredeemed, for they took quite literally the fact that the world depends upon whether or not men love God and do His work. They looked at life not as an exercise in power or a passing pleasure, but as an opportunity to raise all things to God through deeds of daily service. Therefore the great emphasis in the Bible upon the right deed, the holy act. As if life could be violated or hallowed by the will of man and the help of God; as if each act of man either hindered or furthered the redeeming power of God. Creation was not complete, he was taught. God had left it unfinished so that man might seek His partnership in completing it. Upon the pavement of the Roman city of Timgat an inscription was found which reads: "To hunt, to bathe, to gamble, to laugh, that is to live." The Bible is a reminder of the grandeur and the earnestness of living.

A disciple asked his master what the most important thing in the world was. He expected to be told, prayer, study, the Sabbath. Instead the reply he received was—whatever you are dong at the moment! An ancient sage remarked that man should look upon each deed he performs as if it might tip the scales of the world for destruction or redemption. Each deed, even the most trivial, becomes of the highest importance in such a context. Each decision, a decision for God or Satan, an opportunity to hallow life or defile it, a matter of life or death.

There is a special fascination with the Jews today, a consuming curiosity which one beholds everywhere. A case in point is this year's seller; *The Source,* by James Michener, *Herzog* by Saul Bellow, and that of several years ago, *Only in America* by Harry Golden. Three very different books by three very different authors. The first is a panorama of world history written by a Christian Pulitzer prize winner, the second a study in contemporary alienation by perhaps the leading literary virtuoso, the third a heart-warming collection of reminiscenses about the East Side by a home-spun moralist. But all three books have one thing in common—they deal with the Jew! The most memorable Broadway plays during the past few seasons have been Fiddler on the Roof and the Deputy. Two very different plays by two very different playwrights. One is a hilarious musical comedy based on a work by Sholom Aleichem; the other a descent into the depths of tragedy by a German Protestant. But one thing these two plays have in common—they deal with the Jew!

Is it any wonder then that *Time* magazine, in its recent memorable essay on the Jews, said: "The United States is becoming more Jewish. . . . Among American intellectuals the Jew has even become a kind of culture hero. . . . Poet Robert Lowell declared not long ago that 'Jewishness is the theme of today's literature much as the West was in the days of Veblen and the South was in the 30's.' "

Who, one hundred years ago, in the wildest reaches of his imagination, could have believed that all this would be possible? For centuries the Jews were locked up in ghettos, silent, shut off from the outside world that passed them by, an anachronism in the course of history, a fossil that had long ago outlived its usefulness. Now that the ghetto walls have fallen, not only has the Jew emerged into the life stream of the nations, he seems to have become the very symbol, if not the savior, of modern man.

Why? Why the fascination? Why the consuming curiosity? And over books and plays which are, in some cases, quite mediocre. And with a people whose numbers are so ridiculously small that they should have been swallowed up by the grand new life outside the ghetto.

The world finds the Jew fascinating, reads books and attends plays by them and about them, because to the world they are a mystery. The mystery of a people that has faced death and lived, confronted depravity and salvaged decency. For Israel has survived. The ancient scourge, Rome, leveled its cities, destroyed its religion and defeated its God by burning its Temple, slaughtered and enslaved untold numbers, scattering the remnant to the four corners of the world. But the people survived. The modern scourge, Hitler, sent them by the millions into the gas and the flames of Auschwitz and Buchenwald and Belsen. But the people survived.

And not only did they survive facing evil and conquering it physically again and again down the long history of their agony, but what is even more remarkable, they conquered it spiritually. They remained sane. Before Rome drove them into the exile, they had already prepared that amazing world of a book, the Talmud, which became their portable homeland, the source of their wisdom and the blueprint for the fortresses of holiness they built wherever they dwelt. And when the Jews crept forth from the cages and crematoria of Auschwitz, they did not ravage Europe thirsting for revenge, seeking to cut down the "blue-eyed, blond haired Christian devils" of Europe. Instead they quietly went about the excruciatingly difficult task of patiently rebuilding their broken lives, learning new languages, finding new wives and husbands, acquiring new trades, and, miracle of miracles, reestablishing the old-new land of their fathers, the land of Israel.

This is the mystery of Israel—to have faced total annihilation, total evil, total darkness a hundred times, and each time to have surmounted it spiritually and physically, drawing light from darkness and holiness from impurity. It is a mystery because the whole world stands in the very place where Israel stood—on the brink of total annihilation! The growing danger of nuclear war has made of our earth a vast time bomb waiting to explode. There is a frantic search for a way out. But all of the old paths are sealed. There is no escape; no defense. And gradually we seem to be drifting towards a point of no return.

At such a moment in history, when hopelessness envelopes humanity, many have begun to look questioningly at Israel. They seem to say, "You, Israel, you almost alone have stood where all the world now stands; you have tottered on the brink of total annihilation, again and again—and survived—and remained sane. Therefore you must have a message for us. Tell us your secret that we too might live. You, Israel, who have gone through one Auschwitz, the Auschwitz of Hitler, have something to say to us who stand before another Auschwitz, the nuclear Auschwitz."

Israel says that:

> The world is not a derelict which the creator had abandoned to chance. Life . . . is not an opportunity for indulgence, but a mission entrusted to every individual, an enterprise at least as responsible as the management of a factory. Every man constantly produces thoughts, deeds, words, committing them either to the power of holiness or the power of impunity. He is constantly engaged in building or destroying. His task is to

restore, by fulfilling the Torah, what has been impaired in the cosmos, to labor in the service of the cosmos for the sake of God. . . . Scientists dedicate their lives to the study of the habits of insects . . . to them every trifle is significant . . . the Jewish sages investigated just as passionately the laws that ought to govern human conduct. Wishing to banish the chaos of human existence and to civilize the life of man according to the Torah, they trembled over every move, every breath; no detail was treated lightly . . . Perhaps the question of what benediction to pronounce upon a certain type of food, the problem of matching the material to the spiritual, is more important than generally imagined. Man has not advanced very far from the coast of chaos. A frantic call to disorder shrieks in the world. Where is the power that can offset that alluring call? The world cannot remain a vacuum. We are either ministers of the sacred or slaves of evil. The only safeguard against constant danger is constant vigilance, constant guidance.

—Abraham Heschel, *The Earth is the Lords*

Perhaps it is because of this reason that throughout the ages the people of Israel appeared to the other nations as a melancholy people. There was such grief and suffering in their eyes and on their faces, such unending seriousness. And it was so because at least some of them knew the truth. Through the sufferings they endured throughout the ages, at the hands of so many different peoples, they knew the terrible evil within the breast of man. Hitler was no surprise to those who really understood. And the gas chamber and the crematorium was only the ultimate revelation of what potentially existed. They had experienced all this again and again in different fashions and in different ways—in Babylonia, in Alexandria, in Lisbon, in Prague, in London, in Venice, in Kiev, in Warsaw and Berlin—in whatever country they lived. They had experienced it again and again. And therefore they were of the few who took the word of God seriously. It was a harsh word. It was a fearsome word:

If men loved God and obeyed Him, there would be life and blessing; but if they turned away to their own ego, then they would perish.

This was the essence of the word. It was as simple as that. They knew that the world might come to a day of judgment, such as looms ahead of us now.

What Israel is saying is, that if there is no change in the heart of man, then it seems as if an end may come to our world as we know it.

Does that sound fantastic? It is the plain, simple truth, without embellishment or fancy.

How then is it possible that we go about our ways so blissfully complacent, so incredibly oblivious to the reality of the age in which we live? "The strangest aspect of our perilous time is the ominous quiet"—writes atomic scientist, Ralph Lapp. "Probably never in history has the human race looked so much like sheep marching silently to slaughter."

Perhaps we are complacent because reality is incredible.

We live in an Either-Or age.

Either we transform our inner life—*Or* we may perish.

Either we get us a new heart—*Or* we may be turned into ashes.

Either we destroy the idols we worship—*Or* the end may be upon us.

Either we learn to live as brothers under one Father—*Or* we shall devour each other as wild beasts.

It is a time of extremes, an eschatological age.

REPENTANCE

No man repented him of his wickedness, saying, What
have I done?

(Jer. 8:6, 2:13)

To this man will I look,
Even to him that is poor and of a contrite spirit, and
trembleth at my word.
Because thine heart was tender, and thou hast humbled
thyself before the Lord, . . .
And hast rent thy clothes, and wept before me;
I also have heard thee, saith the Lord.
If the wicked will turn from all his sins that he hath
committed,
And keep all my statutes, and do that which is lawful
and right,
He shall surely live, he shall not die.
For I will sprinkle clean water upon you, and you shall
be clean:
From all your filthiness, and from all your idols, will I
cleanse you.
A new heart also will I give you, and a new spirit will I
put within you:
And I will take away the stony heart out of your flesh,
And I will give you an heart of flesh.
And I will put my spirit within you."

(Isa. 66:2; II Kings 22:19; Ezek. 18:21, 36:24-27)

I have a fundamental conviction that a profound psychological reorientation, an experience of conversion, is
needed to get us out of this crisis. What other function do
Judeo-Christian institutions have today, other than to
pray and work for such conversion!

—A. J. Muste

If [disarmament] is to come about, the fundamental
principle on which our present peace depends must be re-
placed by another, which declares that the true and solid
peace of nations consists not in equality of arms but in

mutual trust alone. We believe that this can be brought
to pass . . .

—Pope John, *Pacem in Terris*

You do not stake the life of a great nation on trust.

—Secretary of State Rusk, testifying
in the Senate test ban hearings

It is not easy to realize how many waiting souls there
are in this world. The greater number of men pass
through life with souls asleep. They are like virgins of
the sanctuary who sometimes feel a vague agitation;
their hearts throb with an infinitely sweet and subtle
thrill, but their eyelids droop; again they feel the damp
cold of the cloister creeping over them; the delicious but
baneful dream vanishes; and this is all they ever know of
that love which is stronger than death. . . . That which
has caused the miserable failure of all the efforts of natural
religion is that its founders have not had the courage to
lay hold upon the hearts of men, consenting to no parti-
tion. They have not understood the imperious desire for
immolation which lies in the depth of every soul, and
souls have taken their revenge in not heeding these two
lukewarm lovers.

—Paul Sabatier

Behold, the days come saith the Lord,
That I will make a new covenant with the house of Israel,
    And with the house of Judah:
Not according to the covenant that I made with their
    fathers in the day that I took them by the hand to
    bring them out of the land of Egypt;
Which my covenant they broke, although I was an hus-
    band unto them, saith the Lord.
But this is the covenant that I will make with the house
    of Israel after those days, saith the Lord;
I will put my law in their inward parts, and in their heart
    will I write it;
And I will be their God, and they shall be my people;

And they shall teach no more every man his neighbour,
  and every man his brother, saying, Know the Lord:
For they shall all know me,
From the least of them unto the greatest of them, saith
  the Lord.

(Jeremiah 31:31-34)

In America—today the area of decision in the world of
political reality—I hope for the old, pious, morally radical
forces. There, where men have suddenly come to change
and reflect before, the world situation may make everyone feel the unprecedented responsibility for the course
of mankind—the breath of history and the unique task
within it. A great transforming impulse might jolt the
Americans out of superficial optimism, out of moral
pharisaism, out of the rationalism of know-how, and
awaken them to their own selves. A nation that constitu-
ted its government wisely and successfully, that produced
great statesmen, poets, and theologians, the nation of
Emerson and James, a Western nation, yet more open-
minded than the rest because of its emigrant roots and
ingenuous beginnings—such a nation may yet do the
extraordinary which the life or death of mankind now
depends upon.

Karl Jaspers

Then he answered and spake unto me, saying,
This is the word of the Lord unto Zerubbabel, saying,
Not by might, nor by power, but by my spirit, saith the
  Lord of hosts.

(Zechariah 4:6)

8

Repentance

Realism

I s THIS GREAT mountain of words which I have piled upon these many pages only so much sound and fury? Why engage in such "spiritual" theorizing when the earth itself is at stake? Of what use is this kind of discussion about a change of heart or an inner revolution, since it does not tell one what practical steps are to be taken, what we must "do"?

The approach I am suggesting may even seem amusing to some. Those who find appeals for world law and world government naive yearnings that are removed from the realistic facts of today's situation, and who claim that the present situation only permits the kind of political and military activity which will allow East and West to continue to exist under the present nuclear stalemate, will surely term ludicrous a call to transform the heart of man as the precondition to the success of political or military action.

Let me then review what I have been attempting to say.

I am *not* saying that defense, diplomacy, world law, etc. are of no avail, that we should cease all such efforts and strive to change men's hearts in some global revivalist program.

I *am* saying that in the past all such military, political, and diplomatic efforts were adequate, more or less, to preserve the general society, and that these efforts were helped or hindered by the moral and spiritual level of man at any particular time and place in history. Famine may have ravished lands, tyrants may have enslaved peoples, wars may have brought swift or lingering death to many thousands, but never was man himself in danger. Now a radical change has occurred. Man possesses the power to destroy or radically distort human life, and the probability of such an attempt is close to absolute on the basis of calm, objective analysis of the unrefutable facts. Therefore, even a nuclear ban and world government will not suffice, because the danger is so great and so easily obtainable. Intermediate means, while as necessary now as in the past, are no longer sufficient, for unless an inner change is brought about no outer change can survive.

I am aware that putting the issue in such an absolute form will invite criticisms of irrelevant idealism. I shall be told that if the hope of world government and law are impossible dreams today, how can one speak of the ultimate hope, a change in man's heart and mind; that we must rather engage in a realistic analysis of how to co-exist with Russia under the present conditions.

But to believe that nuclear war will not break out in the next ten to twenty years under the present stalement or even with considerable improvement in international affairs when we know beyond certainty that (1) nuclear power can destroy mankind, (2) it is no scientific secret, (3) it may soon be exceeded in terror by chemical and biological warfare, and (4) if present conditions continue, it is statistically certain, human and mechanical fallibility being what they are, that in time some of these bombs will detonate purposefully or by accident—to believe that disaster will not overtake us in view of these four points is impossible idealism.

All physical scientists know—said Sir Charles Snow— that it is relatively easy to make plutonium. We know this, not as a journalistic fact at secondhand, but as a fact in our experience. We can work out the number of scientific and engineering personnel it needs for a nation-state to equip itself with fission and fission bombs. We know that for a dozen or more states it will take perhaps six years, perhaps less. We know, with the certainty of statistical truth, that if enough of these weapons are made by enough different states, some of them are going to blow up through accident, or folly, or madness—but the motives don't matter. What does matter is the nature of the statistical fact.

In our dilemma, to believe that concentrating on day to day issues alone will prevent the ultimate outburst is illusion; to believe that man's soul can change, and to work toward that change, is the only lasting hope.

The atom bomb, as the problem of mankind's very existence, is equaled by only one other problem—the threat of totalitarian rule (not simply dictatorship, Marxism, or racial theory) with its terroristic structure that obliterates all liberty and human dignity. By one, we lose life; by the other, we lose a life that is worth living. Both extreme possibilities bring us today to an awareness of what we want, how we would wish to live, and what we must be prepared for. The two problems seem fatefully linked. In practice, at least, they are inseparable. Neither one can be solved without the other, and the solution of both calls for forces in man to well up from such depths as to transform him in his moral, rational, political aspects—a transformation so extensive that it would become the turning point of history.

Illusion and tranquillity

"It is astonishing—writes Jaspers—to find this obvious new fact not really acknowledged by people in the world over, least of all in Russia and America. Thus the revolution in our way of thinking, which reflection upon the fact would seem to make inescapable, has not yet occurred. Our attention is distracted, drawn to side issues that are grave but not of absolute moment. Our vision is narrowed as we regard the fact in isolation, though it receives its full view in connection with the entirety of human existence, and with man's questions about himself. We tend to forget, preoccupied as we are with the momentary well-being of economic prosperity.

Our tranquillity in the years before 1914 and 1933 was delusive. Will our present tranquillity continue? Only the unthinking can build their lives on the premise that catastrophe will not occur—or that, if it does, a way out will appear in extremity. To reach true confidence and lend effect to it, we must first destroy all false confidence.

Can we have confidence in technological escape routes from the technological menace? In space, perhaps? No, such ideas belong to the *hubris* of technological omnipotence. Besides, wherever man goes, he will take along his destructive as well as his constructive tools.

Can we trust in the discovery of a kind of antidote to the effect of radioactivity, as defenses have thus far been developed against every offense? Nothing suggests a possibility of effective protection.

There remains the idea of a new Noah's Ark: the artificial reconstruction of our living conditions in huge subterranean shelters that would contain everything required for prolonged subsistence. A remnant of mankind might survive there for decades or generations, until the atmosphere ceased being fatal to the living. Jules Verne thought up a way to do this, critical and inventive engineers, biologists, and physicians would have to test its practicability, and then the politicians would have to decide on the immense expenditures which such preparations for the survival of a few would take. And what then? What would the many do who could not be included in this rescue operation?

Or, we may imagine a political way out and deny that man is doomed unless he changes. We may reason that just because man does not change, there will be no total doom; that things will go on as before, but without world wars; that it is quite possible, even probable, to have the constant threat of war without the reality of it. Fear of the bombs will prevent war: their use is known to be useless, since all would perish and no side would win; growing destructiveness only makes a reckless move less likely. Men will get used to living in a state of undischarged high tension. Why should the balance of terror not last? The argument is that there will be lasting peace—not due to righteousness, nor because the conditions of eternal peace will be met—but because war will be impossible.

There will indeed be a new world situation, but not a new man. The old, unchangeable Adam will renounce war because he must, if not because he ought to. Fear, and the minimum of intelligence it takes to grasp the folly of collective suicide, is motivation enough. How this will affect the present enmity of the totalitarian and free worlds—whether total rule will slowly dissolve from within or be transformed from without— these are matters of political development; whatever happens, they will not affect the exclusion of great-power war from the arsenal of politics. The powers will not acknowledge this exclusion by disarming, for the balance of terror is as indispensable to it as the renunciation of war: the more terror, the less danger of war. Let us just keep going, wait and see, seize our opportunities, act as before, within our limited interests and perspectives. Mankind will not commit suicide.

Such talk has a plausible ring. Of all justifications of confidence, this seems the least illusory. But fear alone cannot bring lasting peace. It is illusory to build a world on fear, on negotiations, and on agreements resting on fear alone. The way out of evil is not that cheap.

Our natural sense of existence also tells us that mankind cannot perish. It says: I cannot believe in this man-made doom in the near future. Something will stop it. Misery, suffering, death are all possible, probably certain—but the total doom of mankind is another matter. I do not believe it.

And again I admit that it is only for moments that I myself can make my heart believe what my mind finds so cogently probable. I must shake myself out of a tendency to reject. Inside us, an original vitality resists and makes us live as if that doom could never be. We want to return to the joy of affirmative existence, and refuse to relinquish it entirely, even when we tear ourselves away and gaze at the gloom.

But against tranquillity stands the experience of this century: more than once the impossible has happened. World War I that removed Europe from the world's center. National Socialism murdered six million Jews. When we first heard of atomic energy, in the twenties, it was a theory, of great interest to our conceptions of matter, but, practically, of no importance. Today they are facts of life.

If tranquillity again threatens to lull us into feeling that a thing is impossible because it is monstrous and beyond the horizon of "normal" concepts, we must ask ourselves why it should be impossible for mankind to perish, and to perish soon? Would it be more monstrous than the fact that man himself is bringing cosmic forces, the sun's own energies, to earth by freeing them from its hitherto tranquil matter?

Aghast, we draw back from finality. It cannot happen. Don't panic! We think this can be handled in a calm atmosphere. Perhaps, however, it is the view of finality and the failure of all direct ways to salvation that will shake men so deeply that they will be changed."

Is it probable that such a transformation can take place? No, it is not "probable"! Such changes have not occurred often in the past, and what is more, the change today must be deeper and more universal than ever before. Then why pursue it? Because there is no other way. To call the step impossible is to pronounce a death-sentence upon mankind, to be carried out within the next hundred years.

I am not attempting to provide any detailed answer to the international diplomacy of our government. I have examined our diplomatic and military attitudes only to show that from every point of view the way seems closed to all those patterns of action which nations have engaged in to settle conflicts and insure survival in the past. Survival can no longer be insured by these means alone. This is what I mean by a radical change and a new epoch in human life. All I wish to do is to show how we can purify the ground from which practical answers may spring forth, how to morally transform men so that they will turn their mind and souls to the real task, and to remind man what he can be. "We do not necessarily have to engage in politics"—writes Jaspers—"but we must arouse that seriousness which can properly motivate seriousness in politics."

We hear the objection that a change in man, who is always an individual, is not a change in politics at large. Great powers that have no common ground as forms of political life, not even in language, are facing each other in the present state of the world with the irreconcilability of mutually exclusive faiths. Even if a change occurred in the politics of one circle, it would still be impossible in the world as a whole because the others are always there too, and vastly powerful; thus we cannot do without the old kind of politics that gets its bearings from force as a last resort. The reform of politics, this argument concludes, has always been an infinite and hence insoluable task; there are no visible indications that the pressure of the new total danger will compel a solution.

We can only answer that if a change in politics should come, it would not come by any objective socio-political process. It would come if the individuals were changed. What will happen to mankind depends upon the individuals who will be standing at the helm in crucial moments. In the final analysis it depends upon all the individuals; what goes on between them lays the foundations of political realities to come.

I do not say a spiritual revolution will take place.

I say that unless it takes place, all other solutions are chimeras.

The proper question to be asked then is, can it happen? And can it happen in such a way as to influence the entire world to move in the direction of permanent peace?

Man can change

Whether or not man can be sufficiently changed and so nurtured as to retain that change is the question which has been asked from the beginning of man. The answer to that question lies in the history of the human race. It is an answer which, in the face of hundred-fold defeat, perilous obstacles, and countless trials, must be affirmative. It *is* possible. Man can change, grow upward, become what he is able to become. The essential message of the Bible for our time, Abraham Heschel reminds us, is not man's discovery of the greatness of God, but God's discovery of the greatness of man. It is upon the deeds of man that God rests His hope, upon the power of man that the glory of God depends. Man is not static, fixed at one immovable point, restricted in his movement and growth. Man is, to the contrary, the freest of all animals. Like a cord tied at two ends, man is bound to the earth through his body and to heaven through his soul. He is partly animal through the physical aspect of his being, and partly angel through the spiritual aspect of his being. He is mortal yet immortal, transient yet eternal, filled at once with misery and grandeur. Like Jacob's ladder, he is fixed into the ground beneath, but his head touches the sky above. The Hebrew word *adam* (man) may be derived from *adamah* which means "dust" or from *d'mut* which means "image." Man is both dust and image. If the image can be distorted, it can seek its true form once again, and raise up even the dust into holy human deeds. Man has the power to become a beast or only a little lower than the angels. There have been, and still are, societies in which spiritual discipline sublimates the desires of man to higher service, where through training and example, common deeds—such as one's daily work, the eating of food, and family life—are so sanctified that man is lifted up to the service of God in that rarest of human phenomena, a community of the faithful. Such societies have always flourished, some for generations, centuries, and even millennia. The Quakers, the Puritans, the Methodists, the Catholics, the Jews and others for longer and shorter periods of time produced such societies.

Man is not only born, he is also nurtured, developed, disciplined, trained. Infinite are the possibilities in man. The Bible holds before us the example of man as he is in the world—in marriage, in work, in government, in society—man who serves God, not in retreat but in community. It contains the record of human creatures, of families, and of an entire people who rose to shimmering heights, as well as the command and the hope for all men.

The road to the renewal of humankind is through the revolution of repentance. Meliorism has deposited us at the precipice, and resignation urges us to step over. These two idolatries have alternated in drawing the loyalty of men's minds, one reacting to the other. I am aware that repentance is not as attractive a formula as might have been brought forth and that it is widely considered a form of self-deception, a kind of revenge upon one's other self, a manner of useless self flagellation, a product of fear or even a psychological malady. Yet the voices which spoke so disdainfully are not as strident today as they were a generation ago. Since then man's self-sufficiency has not brought the millennia; abolishing the divine by way of psychology and enthroning human reason has only compounded the dilemma. The catastrophe that overtook mankind, destroying the idolatry of man's ability to solve all problems, and the approach of another catastrophe have made ready the fertile ground of humility. Without humility there can be no repentance, pride forming the sterile insulation which prevents the self from being judged. The suffering and failure of modern man may have prepared the way, helping to question past idolatries and permitting him to open his soul to that absolute under which he stands in judgment.

Repentance has this power: the power to lay low the evil in man made strong through habit, the power to renew the spirit of man in a way he would not otherwise believe possible. Man is not static, he is dynamic. And though he falls, he possesses the wonderful power to rise and persevere. Furthermore, it is this act of repentance which reveals man's true freedom, freedom to turn from what he believed he was, immovable and unalterable, to become something different and better. It is not enough to say "let us have no regrets" or "just resolve to do better," for where does the strength come from to carry out such resolutions? Every good resolve that does not carry within it the strength for its execution not only causes useless torment but is another defeat. Repentance does contain such strength.

Max Scheler points out that repentance begins with *revulsion*—I did that which was wrong; continues to *knowledge*—I could have done better; then moves into an act of the *will*—I shall do better. This understanding that what we did was wrong, and that we could have done better and shall do so, is the mystery of man's freedom, free to turn away from the past into something new and different. Freedom means new possibilities of achievement formerly undreamt of. And as we rise toward the new self, we are able to look down—like a mountain climber sees the valley below—and view our old self with a curious detachment, as if looking at a different person.

True repentance, however, is not so much something which was done—*conduct*—as about I who could have done that thing—*being*: not "what have I done," but "what kind of person am I that I could have done that!" In other words, not only could we have "acted" differently, we could have "been" different. Such repentance is regret not only for a deed but for ourselves, that "we" could have committed such an act.

In the stirrings of the conscience we become aware of an invisible order, concerning our soul and its relation with its Lord and Creator, which presents itself spontaneously. Repentance thus assumes its full meaning when it no longer strikes at the merely bad, but at the bad which is sin in the eyes of God. As it thus looks up to God, the soul learns to understand the renewal and peace of repentance as the mysterious process known as forgiveness of sin and as an infusion of new strength from the Center of things. Repentance, though it is directed as a personal act against our guilt-laden heart, transcends our heart and looks beyond its impotence to a suspected Center of things, the eternal source of strength. And so every manifestation of this great moral process sets in motion a purposeful reaching out to an invisible world, and if we leave this moment to itself, it will bring before our minds the mysterious outline of an eternal and infinite Judge, an eternal and infinite mercy, an infinite might, an eternal source of life.

Ezekiel spoke of the inner change that would come to his people as a change in heart.

> And I will give them one heart, and I will put a new spirit within you; and I will take the stony heart out of their flesh, and will give them a heart of flesh: that they may walk in my statutes, and keep mine ordinances, and do them: and they shall be my people and I will be their God.
>
> —*Ezek.* 11:19-21

The dialogue of the turning is at the heart of human existence.

God calls to man: "Turn back to me and I will turn again to you."

—*Zech.* 1.3

Man calls to God: "Let me return and I will turn to Thee."

                                                    —*Jer.* 31:18

Martin Buber reminds us that repentance is the translation of the Hebrew, *teshuvah*, which literally means "turning," a turning towards God.

> Turning—he writes—stands in the center of the Jewish conception of the way of man. Turning is capable of renewing a man from within and changing his position in God's world, so that he who turns is seen standing above the perfect zaddik, who does not know the abyss of sin. But turning means here something much greater than repentance and acts of penance; it means that by a reversal of his whole being, a man who had been lost in the maze of selfishness, where he had always set himself as his goal, finds a way to God.

Thus turning is not some physical state, merely an attitude of the soul, but a way of faithful living in the full corporeality of social existence. It is in this sense that we use the word, repentance, as turning. For when man turns away from God, cuts himself off from the source of his life, and endeavors to live a self-sufficient life, he falls into a state of alienation from the root of his life. For the spirit of man lives by the spirit of God, and man dwells not only in the dimension of nature but in a holy dimension which permeates all of life as well.

Now just as there is individual repentance for individual guilt, so is there social or collective repentance for the guilt of an entire society. Who is not involved in the catastrophe of our own time? Germans? The first words spoken by Karl Jaspers, the exiled German thinker, when he returned to lecture at a German university after the war, were: "The very fact that you and I are alive means that we are guilty!" Americans? We were the ones to first explode the bomb, and even now all these years after it was used there has been no great movement on the part of individuals in this country to express our shame. Russians? Chinese? French?

Max Scheler's words are strangely prophetic:

> We see in history how repentance can grow into a mighty torrent; how it rushes for a generation through

whole peoples and civilizations; how it opens obdurate hearts to compassion; how it historically illumines the past of nations which was hidden by racial pride; how it broadens the once ever narrowing future into a broad, bright plane of possibilities—and so prepares the way for regeneration of a collective moral existence. Such process of communal repentance—for an accumulation of communal guilt—reoccurs with a rhythm of its own throughout the history of nearly all great communities . . . It was not least through the invincible tears of its repentance that early Christianity renewed the out-going world of antiquity, hardened by pleasure seeking, by lust and power and glory, and poured into that world a feeling of rejuvenation. . . . Yet another mighty wave of repentance ran through the peoples of Europe after the increasingly savage, life-destroying brutality of the Eleventh Century had taken hold . . . , constriction, paralysis and cultural fragmentation, then once again resolution through repentance and reacceptance of the old ingredients into a new creative will to life and spirit of total rebirth; it is not only the little individual soul which breathes in this rhythm, but the great soul of mankind in history.

Borne on a wave of repentance, that conversion will also come to pass which is intrinsically the sole condition for the formation of the new political system of European union. No new juristic, no diplomatic good will, not even any "revolution" nor any "new men" can take the place of this *change of heart* among the peoples. . . . The necessary form of consciousness, out of which alone can be borne new positive attitudes and finally new plans of political reconstruction, is that recent feeling of profound *revulsion.*   —Max Scheler, *On the Eternal in Man*

Scheler spoke of the revulsion which spread over post-World War I Europe. What would he have said of the hundred-fold revulsion erupting in men's hearts today, the indictment under which they stand for having permitted the dream of God to be turned into a nightmare? Modern man knows the feeling of being indicted before God, of being held to account for the gift of life given to him. There is a sense of judgment above the heads of every man who ceases to deceive himself and faces the sentence of his own soul.

In the past, folly and wickedness had limited consequences; today they draw all mankind to perdition. Now, unless all of us live with and for one another, we shall all be destroyed together. This new situation demands a corresponding solution. It is not enough to find new institutions; we must change ourselves, our characters, our moral-political wills. What used to distinguish individuals, to be effective in small groups but impotent in society at large, has now become a condition for the continued existence of mankind.

I do not think I am exaggerating. Whoever goes on living as before does not comprehend the menace. Mere intellectual speculation about it does not mean absorption into the reality of one's life—and the life of man is lost without a change. Man must change if he wants to go on living. If he thinks only of today, a day will come when the outbreak of nuclear war is apt to finish everything.

What are the facts of today? Political motivation does not reach far enough, but as yet we see no change in ethical motives either. Man is still the same as ever. We see the same violence, ruthlessness, belligerent recklessness, coupled with the same indolence and indifference, the same desire for quiet and lack of provident concern in those who happen to be well off at the moment. We see the same brazen blackmail and the submission to it, the same hiding behind a fictitious authority which some secretly despise, others regard as a guarantee of their comfort, and all will forsake at the decisive moment.

The change can come only in every man's manner of living. Every act, every word, every attitude matters. What happens on a large scale is but a symptom of what is done in the privacy of many lives. The man who cannot live in peace with his neighbor, the mischief-maker or secret ill-wisher or slanderer or liar, the adulterer or undutiful son or negligent parent or lawbreaker—by his conduct, which even behind locked doors is never wholly private—keeps peace from the world. He does, in miniature, what makes mankind destroy itself on a larger scale. Nothing that man is and does is quite without political significance.

The actions of statesmen also need the ethical illumination. That is our premise for the survival of mankind. A man may have delivered the most eloquent moral-political speeches at the conference table; if he is faithless at home, he shares the blame for the continuing evil. If he is so tolerant of human failings as to allow loose-living individuals in his official domain, he undermines the trustworthiness of the whole. If he wants the miracle to happen, if he wants an ethical change, and still lets the world carry on unthinkingly, he makes ethics itself suspect. And so it goes: talking, negotiating, enterprising, organizing, until the day when everything will be erased.

We may ask how "private" conduct can affect political action. The question rightly points to the absence of a direct causal link, but it fails to recognize that a man's private life is a symptom of his personality, which is the same in whatever sphere he may move. It is opportunism which, in one sphere, lets him obey rules he may flout in others. A stockbroker keeps his word because one failure to do so would finish him in his profession. The politician follows the rules of an international community because the consequences of violating them under normal conditions would be too unpleasant. But the dictates of opportunism and convention do not hold in matters of life or death. The motivations of men at such times cannot be special ones, kept in abeyance for the day of need. They will work only if they have been working for a lifetime, in politically harmless circumstances and in the entire life of the individual. The moral idea is one and indivisible.

As everything that can be planned becomes political, we may think that we need something we cannot plan. And indeed, there is no concrete answer to the question: "What should we do?" There are only the ancient prophets to remind us of potentialities now dormant. What we need now, in the face of extremity, is more than a better insight: it is a change of heart. But this change cannot be forced.

We can point out realities and sound the call of thousands of years ago. Both the possibilities of the future and the demands of that prophetic voice should permeate our schools, though even among the young the results, if any, are left to the freedom of every individual. If the basic facts of our

political existence are laid bare and the consequences of vary-
ing conduct set forth, the answer must come from the individual—not in an opinion but in his life.

Is it possible for man to change? Was he not always the
same in the thirty or fifty centuries of his known history and,
by inference, in those that went before? History teaches that
anything great made by men was soon destroyed by men. On
grounds of experience we can expect no change.

This thesis is true enough for the natural makeup of man
as one living creature among others. But it ignores the
phenomenon that makes man truly human, more than a
zoological species; unaltered in his psychophysical constitu-
tion, man does, in recurrent changes, transform his historical
appearance. All that is great, luminous, and inspiring has
risen—against all experience and over all that keeps dragging
us down—from a different source. Historically, in spite of
what biology and psychology can comprehend, a change in
man is possible. It happened with the Hebrew prophets, with
the Greek poets and philosophers, with the Hellenistic and
Christian regenerations of the first centuries A. D., with the
biblically grounded ethics of the Protestant world. Each of
these transformations, while withering in time, has remained
a challenging memory.

The hardest task to be performed anew by every individual
—a task which no man can do for another—has always been to
come to himself in extremity, to be changed, and then to be
guided in life by the impulses springing from the change.
At first, the fact of the bomb can shock only individuals into a
reflection radical enough to make them live henceforth in an
earnestness commensurate with the two present tasks of mankind: salvation from total rule and salvation from total destruction. And nothing short of this earnestness is adequate
to our eternal task of growing truly human.

The great turning of individual man can also become a
great turning of communities and even nations, turning from
the fragmented lives of self-sufficiency back to confrontation
with the infinite.

"Repent one day before you die," an ancient sage taught.
"But how do we know when we shall die?" the students
replied. "Perhaps we shall die tomorrow." "Just so," replied

the sage. "Since a man may indeed die on every morrow, let each day of his life be a day of repentance."

Such a teaching is part of the treasure house of man's wisdom, and wise men have understood what simple men did not. For simple men understand that they would live differently if they knew that their days were numbered. Why argue, why be petty, why hold grudges, why be small—if death is on the doorstep? Most men in such circumstances grow an inch or two taller (some, of course, are destroyed) and live far nobler for the remaining weeks and months than all the years before. They draw upon a perspective which they always possessed but rarely used, the ability to distinguish that which is apparent from that which is real, that which is important from that which is trivial, that which is passing from that which is lasting. They reject the apparent, the trivial, the passing, and seek the real, the important, the lasting. But we rarely are given to know when we are to die, and so we have no use for that proper perspective and, as a result, are slaves of the moment rather than servants of the eternal.

Now the wise men of all ages did not need the fear of imminent death to stir them to noble deeds. They were always aware of the precious moments of life, that man's origin is dust and he returns to the dust, "that his days are like the grass that withers, the flower that fades, the fleeting shadow, the passing cloud, the floating dust, the dream that vanishes." The wise man lives always as if the next day were the last, and thus all his days are nobility and wisdom.

But, strange to say, today the wise man and the simple man are one. Today we all agree that the presence of death is not simply an "as if" presence theoretically posited to turn us to better living. Now our flesh prickles at the angel of death who awaits us. We know he is there. He flutters about our earth, at times seeming to envelop it in his grasp; only obtuseness of soul has closed our ears to the flapping of his great wings and to the eerie screech of his voice.

There are those who will say, yours is a pessimistic thesis. For what you are saying is that our scientific revolution demands such spiritual excellence that the smallest deviation can destroy us. But history proves that spiritual excellence is virtually unattainable and if attainable, only for short periods of time with many deviations. Therefore you give the world little hope.

I do not disagree with this analysis. I only wish to act on the basis of it, and not on some chimera. The evidence of the new and the old—modern science and the ancient prophetic word—is so stark and clear that it should bring a shaking of the foundations. Indeed, unless those foundations are shaken, even they may disappear.

BIBLICAL FAITH
AND MODERN MAN

I went to call on the Lord in His house on the high hill,
My head full of one-hundred-and-fifty million, having to
    grow up overnight.
"If ever a people, Lord, needed a miracle!"
The Lord looked at me as a mountain might look at a
    molecule.
"So you want a miracle," said the Lord. "My! My! You
    want a miracle.
I suppose you mean that you want me to come sliding
    down a sunbeam and make one-hundred-and-fifty mil-
    lion self-willed egotists overnight into one-hundred-and-
    fifty million cooperative angels.
Brother," said the Lord, in a voice that shook the
    windows, "That isn't the sort of universe you're living
    in.
And that isn't the sort of God I am."
The room was suddenly vast, with the stars set bright in
    the ceiling.
"There is only one miracle," said the Lord.
"All else is cause and effect. All else is law."
The thunder withdrew from the Voice, and the words
    came hushed and clear
Like the first stars in the twilight, each star a newborn
    glory.
"There is only one miracle, and it is already accomplished.
That miracle is the human soul."
The Lord He lifted His head and the Milky Way was
    His hair.
"The soul is like the atom," He said. "Wonderfully like
    the atom.
Consider the atom.
So minute no lens you can make can enlarge it to a point
    where your eye can see it, yet there's a whole solar
    system inside it, whirling around a nucleus like the
    planets around the sun,
So feeble in its unreleased state, yet actually the greatest
    force, save one, in creation,
The greatest force in creation, save one."
"I have given you a soul," cried the Lord, "and you ask
    Me to come down and do a magician's trick!

The people who smashed the atom didn't beg Me to
to come with a thunderbolt and split the nucleus for
them.
They knew that there is power in the atom and they set
to work to release it.
They succeeded, and shook not only New Mexico, they
shook the world.
All they had to do was to get past the electrons, crack
the nucleus, and release the power waiting to be used.
"There is power in the human soul," said the Lord,
"When you break through and set it free,
 Like the power of the atom.
More powerful than the atom,
It can control the atom,
The only thing in the world that can.
I told you that the atom is the greatest force in the world,
save one.
That one is the human soul.

"But," said the Lord—and the stars in the sky seemed to
stand still and listen——
"The power must be released, as the atom-breakers released the power of the atom.
They had to get past the electrons to get at the energy
packed in the nucleus. . . .

The Lord He looked at me and His eyes pierced like
hot wires.
"Perhaps," He said, "there's something in you and
numerous others that will have to be cracked open,
if a hundred-and-fifty million people are going to grow
up overnight.
Something in you," said the Lord, "something, perhaps,
in you."

That was a joke, and I laughed. But the Lord wasn't
laughing.
I hastened to reassure Him. There's nothing the matter
with me.
It's the other fellow that's the trouble, a hundred-and-
fifty millon of him."

"I know all about the hundred-and-fifty million," said
the Lord, and I thought He seemed a little tired as
He said it, "but I don't at the moment seem able to
see anyone but you."
"Me, Lord?" I said. "How odd! I'm sure you must
be mistaken.
There's nothing about me that need give you even a
moment's uneasiness."

—Herman Hagedorn

We have just enough religion to make us hate, but not
enough to make us love one another.

—Swift

Disbelief in Christianity is not so much to be dreaded
as its acceptance with a complete denial of it in society
and politics.

—M. Rutherford

If Christianity refuses to realize social justice on the
assumption that the sinfulness of human nature makes
it impossible, the task will be undertaken by that
sinful nature without its help, and the idea of justice
will be distorted and spoiled.

—Berdyaev

Let justice well up as waters
And righteousness as a mighty stream.

(Amos 5:24)

9

Biblical Faith and
Modern Man

Does this mean that Biblical faith has nothing more specific to say to modern man than a call to repentance? The answer is both negative and positive: negative if we are thinking of repentance as merely a disembodied state of the soul; positive if we understand repentance as the turning point of one's existence, a new attitude toward life itself. Biblical religion can speak directly to present needs. I know of no better recent statement to introduce my own observations than that of Dr. Louis Finkelstein:

> To few generations, if any, including their own, could the message of the prophets of Israel apply so directly as it does to us. Substitute Moscow for Babylonia, and Assyria; when you read what is said of Jerusalem, think of New York and Washington, and you find that the prophets are describing the perils and the circumstances of our life today. We are in mortal peril, but seem to be able to drown our worries in a round of pleasure-seeking,

power-seeking, and immediate satisfaction of material wants; and that was precisely the situation in ancient Israel and Judah. The prophets tried to persuade the people to take their situation seriously and to come to the heart of their problem. And the heart of the problem is not in Washington or Moscow, but in the personal lives of each of us. If we all go about our business as usual, we must expect the governments of the earth to do the very same, seeking power, aggrandizement, petty victories, which can lead only to the grave, precisely as we do in our private lives. For the mere fact that Johnson lives in the White House, and Kosygin in the Kremlin, has not changed their character; they are what we are, people struggling for apparent achievement, while real achievement is eluding them.

In the nature of things it must elude them. We are asking of each of our rulers the impossible. They have attained their positions, each in his own way, through competition, a certain ruthlessness toward their opponents, a delight in battle, and an ability to over-ride opposition. After their arrival at supreme power, we except them suddenly to change, as by a miracle, and to become sages and saints, worried about the survival of man, rather than about their own role in the passing scene.

If one reads Amos, Hosea, Joel, Isaiah, Jeremiah or Ezekiel, one comes to a new world and new insights. These men were concerned not with the next election, not with the opposition to them, not with budgets, not with victory over other men, but with the character of man. For them, the question was not "Will we survive?" but "Do we deserve to survive?"

So the prophets would have been as concerned about juvenile delinquency in New York, Chicago, and Philadelphia, as about the atomic or the hydrogen bomb. They would have been more worried about our souls, than about our bodies. They would have been more frightened at the thought of inflicting injustice and committing murder, than at the thought of suffering injustice and of being murdered.

The John Birch Society, desiring to impeach Chief Justice Warren for the effort of the Supreme Court under him to bring about the equalization of white and Negro, and the defense of the underprivileged, is as great a danger to our nation as either the Russians or the Chinese can be, no matter how they may be armed. Corrupt politicians, corrupt labor leaders, and immoral businessmen threaten this nation's security more than does any enemy.

While the world in which they the prophets lived was shaking, they could only sing one song: try to live as civilized human beings, try to live rationally, try to be unafraid, try to think of your apparent enemy as your brother, who is misled. What they asked of their generation, and what they ask of us, is very difficult to achieve. In crisis men may reach new heights of nobility or sink into an abyss of infamy. . . .

Arm yourselves with deterrent bombs by all means. Strengthen your defenses. Preserve Zion as inviolable, says Isaiah. But before you do so, make sure that it ought to be inviolable. Are people in your country treated as chattels? asked Jeremiah of the people of Jerusalem. Your first duty is to free them; then you have a right to resist the Babylonians. Would he not say the same to us? Do you place a higher value on delightful ornaments and personal comfort than you do on the education of your children, your own education, and above all your own righteousness? Then, says Isaiah, you are engaged in the aboriginal biological warfare of the survival of what Darwin calls the fittest, but really means the strongest. Other species have disappeared from the earth; and so may we.

Are politics in New York City corrupt? Do we honor people who have made money, no matter how they made it? Do we encourage youth to seek success at any cost; and young girls to prize popularity above decency and even chastity? Do we regard the men who are trying to serve God as freaks and weaklings, to be despised? Are we diverting energies intended to make man better into efforts simply to have him live a few more miserable years? Is our charity and philanthropy given to men of power rather than to God? Do we begrudge the success of our nearest neighbor, or even of our brother? Or even our spouse? Or our child or father or disciple? Are we more deeply moved by hatreds than by loves? If we do any of these things, we are human, in the sense of being dominated by emotions, but that part of the human condition is shared by virtually the whole animal kingdom.

But if Jerusalem could be called the city of righteousness, the struggle between Israel and Assyria would become a struggle between God and the kingdom of arrogance. In such a struggle the kingdom of arrogance might for the moment appear victorious; but it could only be for the moment, for God's kingdom is everlasting. Arrogance wins battles; it always loses wars.

"Not 'Will we survive?' but 'Do we deserve to survive?' " asks Rabbi Finkelstein. This is the ultimate question. The question before which all other questions—military, diplomatic, and moral—bow. It is the question posed by the man of faith, who alone penetrates the inner essence of our agony. It is a question etched out in all its manifold power and illumined in all its awesome wonder in a remarkable passage from the modern Christian martyr, Whittaker Chambers:

> "Father, what am I to answer those people who keep writing me that I was wrong to write in *Witness* that I had left the winning side for the losing side? They say that by calling the West the losing side, I have implied that evil can ultimately overcome good."
>
> Father Alan studied his hands, which were lying in his lap. Then he glanced at me directly and asked: "Who says that the West deserves to be saved?"
>
> If, in that softly lighted room, Father Alan had burst a Verey flare, he could scarcely have lit up more effectively the ravaged landscape of that No Man's Land across which the West confronts its crisis, supposing that it is only an alien enemy it confronts, not knowing that the enemy it confronts is first of all itself.

... Father Alan's question cut past the terms in which men commonly view the crisis of our time. It cut past all ratios of opposed power, past the armaments race and the production race, past the atomic weapons, bombs, and the bombers, the guided missiles and the craftily guided policies, the marshalled divisions and the marshalled statistics. It did not ask: Has the West the physical power to survive? It asked: Is the West justified in surviving? Does the West retain within itself what alone in life and history ever justifies the survival of anything, and which is ultimately a play of creative force whose test and whose mandate is that it impels men to die for it, not because they wish to die, but because they feel its shaping power so completely that they would rather die than live without it? So long as men identify themselves with that force to the point where they will to die for it, it is living and provides that inner certitude, greater and more instant than any idea or reasoning, which holds nations upright as they pick up momentum in the terrifying slopes and turns of history. The moment men in masses begin to question that force, at that moment it has begun to die. However long the tremor of its decay may take, time will henceforth be no more than a delay. Every civilization embodies a certain truth to which it gives reality. When that truth, which is, in turn, embodied in a faith held religiously whether or not it is wholly religious—when that faith loses its power to inspire men, its downfall is at hand. When that faith and that truth no longer match and meet the reality of men's daily lives, there sets in a radical readjustment of reality whereby men seek to bring the faith by which they live into conformity with the reality they live in. Thus every social revolution begins with a spiritual and intellectual revolution. Men revolt first in thought, in order to be free to revolt in act. But revolt does not always imply violence. It may simply take the form of a question. When the gap grows too clear between the faith and forms of a civilization and the realities of daily life, masses of men are paralyzed by the discrepancy so that before the old faith they first grow numb, then apathetic, then questioning, if not disdainful. They simply by-pass in one degree or other, what no longer corresponds to their reality. It has lost its power to inspire their lives. This happens even if they continue outwardly to conform to the old ways. This is the real crisis of the West and the point at which, across a No Man's Land of apathy, it confronts itself. Communism is only a secondary manifestation of this crisis although Communism has reached a strength where it complicates and threatens to solve in its own terms the crisis of the divided West. For Communism is not an Asiatic or Russian growth, as some maintain. In its Soviet form, it has been shaped and colored by Russian peculiarities. But Communism is a way of thought and action, a way of reading history and its forces, which was developed in the culture capitals of the West. The growth of its power is inexplicable except as Communism appeals to the divided mind of the West, making each of its advances exactly along the line of the West's internal division, paralyzing each effort of the West to cope with it by touching some sympathetic nerve. The success of Communism, as I have written elsewhere, is never greater than the failure of all other faiths.

—Chambers, *Cold Friday*

The ringing tone of these prophetic outcries sounds so strangely sane, calling out to mind and heart at once, cutting through human divisiveness, and revealing the common core of spiritual concern which if recognized, could revolutionize our world. The challenge facing modern man has joined as allies those who formerly went separate ways. The religious faiths of the West, Judaism and Christianity—itself split into Catholic and Protestant divisions—have had their disputations in the past, the echoes of which are not yet stilled, but these quarrels, legitimate though they may be, grow dim before the looming perils of Russia and the Bomb, joining the disciples of Biblical faith in defense of that image of God which they alike believe man supremely symbolizes. In theory none would dare deny this brotherhood, this solemn unity in the face of overwhelming, diabolical terror; all would cry folly at the disunity of the Biblical faiths at such a juncture in history. Yet, desperate as is the need for a program of joint concern and common action which would effectively harness the untold power of the spirit and the mind and provide, if properly directed, that energy with which Western man may learn to build those foundations upon which the free world will establish its existence, and without which it cannot long persist—there has been no radical change of alignment or concern.

Let me list several of the practical areas of action where Biblical faith can and must speak to Western man, and to the entire world.

Patience

We Americans grow impatient as time goes on and no simple solution is to be found to the nuclear dilemma, no easy victory over Russia, but, to the contrary, we continue to lose ground not only scientifically and geo-politically, but "prestige-wise," missing the friendship of countries we have given billions to and losing the votes of U. N. neutrals. We are impatient already. For the first time in our history we have begun to feel that time is not necessarily working for us, as it always has in the past, but against us. We do not take easily our change of role from "liberator" to "colonialist," from the land of the free to the nation where only the white man is free, from frontiersmen to calculating industrialists, from idealists to reactionaries. Unused to the fine arts of diplomacy and power-politics which European nations have practiced for centuries, a deepening sense of frustration seizes us as we assess our position. Accustomed to achieve and achieve quickly, what we seek, indefinite stalemate may be more than we can sustain. Thrown into one crisis after another in Laos, Congo, Cuba, Berlin, and Vietnam, with continued setbacks and no sign of relief, we may be tempted to take extreme positions of easy war or easy peace in search of a quick solution.

On the one hand, a crescendo of voices from representative sections of the population are now heard, urging the government to settle matters once and for all. The John Birch Society, and a surprisingly large number of sympathizers, who want America to take such steps as might set off nuclear war, because of defense of "honor" and "liberty," tell us that we have been pushed around enough and that our nation's freedom demands immediate and limitless action. Recent novels and films describe nuclear war beginning in this way, through some atomic Oswald emerging unexpectedly to assassinate mankind. The movement toward the radical right, which prepared the ground for one presidential candidate, is a constant threat to an impatient land, accustomed to quick victories.

On the other hand, it is becoming increasingly clear that the principles which justified wars in the past—liberty and honor—may themselves be destroyed in this next war. For if there is no semblance of human civilization left, there can be neither liberty nor honor, and war itself becomes impossible. As a result of this line of thinking, which is difficult to refute and is molding the opinions of more and more Americans as months pass, megation power increases, the danger of war mounts, and all these facts and their logical consequences are permitted to sink into the consciousness of the American mind—a movement toward easy peace grows. A mood of despair settles upon us as Russia moves ahead in country after country, as neutral nations align themselves with the East, and as the U. N. is weakened. The phrase "better red than dead"—the belief that anything is better than war, even surrendering to Russia on unconditional terms—may become a popular cry in this land of the brave and home of the free, as it already is in Britain and Germany.

Against both solutions, easy war and easy peace, Biblical faith must counsel patience and courage.

Patience is required to keep from giving way to simple answers, because neither man nor history is simple. The ambiguous nature of man and history is a profound lesson of the Bible. The world is unredeemed, yet redemption is always possible; man falls, yet he may at any time rise and mount onward. History is not progress, and man is not an angel. There is retrogression and there is the demonic as well. Patience is found in strength not of limbs but of spirit, in the knowledge that the spirit of the Lord still hovers above the deep, that man is anchored at the depths of his being in a holy dimension of reality which may yet pervade our world. "In the place where there are no men", taught an ancient sage, "be thou a man."

Responsibility

Though nuclear war seems inevitable through the explosion of one or more bombs within a few years either through design or accident, nevertheless, the fact is that no bomb has yet exploded since Hiroshima.

No bomb has yet been exploded.

Biblical faith denies that man is helplessly encircled by the hands of fate. It asserts that man is responsible for his past, his present, and his future. Man has brought the world to this impasse, and if the bombs are dropped, man will drop them. The greatest danger confronting us is the creeping paralysis of despair.

The world was placed into man's hands; he has the power to kill or to keep alive, to tear down or to build up. Created to rule the earth, man was given a mind to think with, a conscience to feel with, a law to live by, and the presence of the divine to guide him. But God will not act for him. Man alone possesses the power and the choice.

Every individual knows that he must die, even though he must live as if it were not so. That each man will die is certain. That mankind will die is not certain. It is possible, even probable, but not certain, not the unalterable result of some objective natural law. Whether or not mankind will perish depends upon mankind itself.

The Doomsday Bomb, or whatever mechanical monster will turn our earth into cinder and smoke, is therefore not some irresistible force which is almost upon us, resistance to which is hopeless and which must be accepted with final resignation. Every step on the road to disaster depends on the men who take it: the discovery of natural phenomena as well as their translation into technology, the order to make the bombs as well as the order to drop them and its execution. We must recognize the difference between man's work, which is up to us, and the work of nature, which we can master only to a degree. We dare not fail in the work that is ours by submitting to "fate" from the outset. If we are to fulfill the obligation of our freedom, we dare not renounce it by premature surrender.

Biblical faith must never permit man to despair. There is no fate. There is only man's will, God's word and the world.

Greatness

Biblical faith must not only remind man of his responsibility and counsel patience, it must awaken him to his capacity for greatness. We have seen the beast in man; we need to be told of the divine image that dwells within. The great revelation of the Bible is not the depravity of man, but his glory. That creature—almost divine—who alone joins heaven and earth, finitude and infinity, body and soul, the one who alone hears and can respond to the divine word, the one who dreams and yearns, who loves truth and hates falsehood, who is able to redeem, return, and renew—is man.

If the powers of evil can dehumanize man until his depravity threatens to cancel human history, then we must recall the powers of holiness that can likewise redeem him. Man's noblest possession and most sacred task is to lift up all of life to God, to ennoble days and hours, to sublimate passion and power in the service of the Highest, in a word, to sanctify life.

Biblical faith teaches us that God created the world and fashioned man in His own image, that He has given man the power to discover God's will and to obey it, and that man's task, therefore, is neither to escape from the world nor to worship it as it is, but, with God's word and man's deed, to fulfill God's dream for His creation. It says that we have the power of hallowing the natural desires of man, that we can find a way of ennobling and raising prosaic acts which lend them meaning and significance, an aspect of holiness, that we may succeed in transforming them into a means of serving God. The glory of man is the power to hallow, for in hallowing life he becomes holy.

Concerning Abraham's receiving the three angels and preparing a meal for them, it is written, "And he stood above them, under the tree, and they did eat" (Gen. 18:8). Puzzled by this verse, a disciple of a famous sage asked him if it was not strange that Scripture should say that the man stood above the angels.

No, the wise man explained. It was not strange at all. The angels are superior to man, but man is also superior to the angels. The angels are superior to man because they are pure and not a part of the natural world. Man is superior to the angels because, though he is part of nature, he possesses the power to hallow and raise up to God the common, natural acts of which the angels know nothing. This verse is an example of that. The angels have no need of food and thus, even though they are pure, they are ignorant of the manner of hallowing the act of eating. But Abraham was a man who knew that even by the way in which we approach our food, we can serve the Almighty. Thus, in this case, when he invited them to his table for a meal, Scripture speaks the truth: he stood above them.

The man who finds his way to God in the midst of the world is greater than the angels. The angels may be pure because they are apart from our world; they come from heaven and are innocent of the tasks, the problems, and vexations that confront man. They are static; they neither rise nor fall in their everlasting splendor. But man comes from earth as well as heaven; he possesses a body as well as a soul; he has evil thoughts as well as good ones; he knows passion and greed as well as justice and mercy. He is never static but rises and falls, is capable of turning into a beast or the most glorious of creatures. Man can be purer than the angels because he—and only he—is called upon to raise earth to heaven. Man can rise higher than the angels because his task is greater than theirs—to hallow all of life, to conduct his business with honesty, to be gentle with his wife and children, to fight for good government, to treat his fellowman as he would be treated, to curb jealousy and desire, and to act in such a way that all his deeds become holy deeds, all his actions holy actions, even the commonest of them.

Purpose

In a series of articles in the *Manchester Guardian Weekly*, D. W. Brogan observes "a steady deterioration in American self-confidence and trust in the 'American way of life.'" Mr. Brogan noted that the Russian lead in space exploration has Americans worried.

But—he continues— . . . the irritation and malaise that I encountered have deeper roots than apprehension at the state of the national defenses. It is more a matter of the whole moral tone of the American way of life than immediate deficiencies that an intelligent administration can cure.

As indices to this "moral tone," Mr. Brogan lists scandal in government, police corruption, price-fixing in the electrical and drug industries, the crime rate, the school system, the John Birch Society, etc.

All these causes of frustration and irritation—Mr. Brogan concludes—explain to some extent the failure of the President to get from Congress the means of improving the American image and giving effect to relevant American policy.

Biblical faith can recall this country to its national purpose. It can help instill that sense of meaning into the people of the United States which would purify its communal life, multiply its strength and guarantee a willingness to sacrifice. It can use the challenge of world crisis to turn men's concern inward, urging them to begin with their own land, their own city, their own community—themselves. To recall America to its true purpose means talking bluntly and acting bluntly, sweeping away the smoke-screen of the *status quo* that has been accepted as normality in an environment so poisoned with pleasure-seeking, conniving, and outright immorality that it threatens to smother us all. It means preaching and practicing the prophetic demands. The ten commandments would be a good place to begin: idolatry, hypocrisy, honesty, responsibility, fidelity. What a program could be drawn up!

Dare spiritual leaders counsel the nation how to conduct itself in the frightful Russian nuclear stalemate without at the same time, and as a necessary prerequisite, sweeping away the corruption and decay that surrounds our own commonwealth, without helping to prepare the United States for the terrible trial it faces and will continue to face by establishing that moral health without which we may defeat ourself? "The indifference of believers," said Father Yelchaninov, "is something far more dreadful than the fact that unbelievers exist." Bad government, local, state and national, family delinquency, slums, race-prejudice, and moral breakdown are not insolubles. Their solutions are bound up with solutions to international problems. If the world is sick, one of the first steps must be to heal ourselves.

American religion should turn to these problems with all the energy at its command. If it did, the epidemic of moral breakdown could be halted. If the power of the pulpit were put to its proper use, there are few cities which could not control its criminal element and conduct its government in a manner compatible with its purpose, instead of maintaining the present level of corruption which gives politics so negative an association that many true leaders are often discouraged from seeking office.

Rome was no more ripe for defeat than are we. And we could do with a few twentieth century Savanarolas. It is unbelievable that religion today conducts itself in a "business as usual" manner: sermons, lectures, ritual, protocol—in a word "religion"—as if nothing had really changed. Otherwise, how is it that the organized power of religion is so seldom used in behalf of a *local* righteous cause. "With most people" said Vivekananda, "religion is a sort of intellectual assent and goes no further than a document. I would not call it religion. It is better to be an atheist than to have that sort of religion."

At this time of crisis spiritual leaders of all faiths must become messengers of the living God, standing witness to Him amidst the idolatries of men. What the leaders of religion need at this crucial hour is the depth of learning, the certainty of conviction, and the readiness to serve with every bit of strength come what may. Their sermons should be fire, their prayers tears, and their actions the sure strokes of a mighty hammer, smashing the false, the cheap, and the tawdry, and building nail by nail, board by board, the temple of the Lord.

Once Rabbi Akiba went with a delegation of five rabbis on a mission to Rome. It was at the beginning of the second century and Rome was still in its full power. They took him on a tour of the city. They showed him their bridges and their bath houses, their art galleries and their circuses, their museums and their military outposts, their statues and their palaces. Then they said to him proudly:

"Are you impressed?"

Akiba replied:

"No."

They were shocked.

Akiba explained:

"When we were walking in the square we saw a splendid statue of the Emperor. And as we went by it began to rain. I saw the slaves who were on duty guarding the statue take velvet robes and cover it so that it would not get wet, and I saw the slaves who covered the staute with velvet robes were wearing rags. I am not impressed with Rome. For a city in which statues wear robes and human beings wear rags cannot long endure."

This, in one sentence, is the task in our time:

To remind a country gone mad of the true values.

To remind a nation which loves things and uses people that God wants us to love people and use things.

To remind a nation drunk with vanity and eager for pleasure of the need to respect each human being.

Drug stores sell fifty million dollars worth of tranquilizers each year because, in this pleasure-mad society, man cannot rest. Religion in our age must not be a tranquilizer but a goad, calling out in the name of God for justice and compassion.

Ours is a society prosperous but uneasy, which spends millions on entertainment, and yet still cannot sleep; which pushes, bribes, and drives to get ahead, yet does not know where to go. Religion in our time must teach us that money is the passport to every place but heaven, that it can buy anything but happiness, and that, without purpose and dedication and self control, our nation cannot endure.

Religion in our time must be a challenge to understand life not only in terms of what I can get out of the world, but also in terms of what the world will get out of me.

Religion in our time must cease being convenient and comfortable, asking nothing and giving everything, closing its eyes to hypocricy within its own walls. It must discipline, set standards, make demands, and it must not be afraid to level judgment when necessary and to accuse, to stand witness in the name of the Almighty against he mounting fraud which threatens to suffocate us, crying out with the prophet,

Woe unto them that call evil good and good evil; that change darkness into light and light into darkness.

(Isaiah 5:20)

Sacrifice

If the national purpose of our land and ourselves as individual Christians and Jews were clear, if we believed in that purpose truly and strongly, and if we wanted to further that purpose, then, it would seem to me, we would be willing to discipline ourselves to sacrifice for the sake of others.

The problem of the underdeveloped nations looms before the world, exposing them to influences which may subvert their faith to satisfy the need for food, and lead to injustice and inequality. What would happen if the United States would begin to spend on a number of underdeveloped countries what American Jews are spending on Israel or America itself on Puerto Rico—something like one thousand dollars per citizen—enough to clothe, house, and usefully train almost the entire population? Of course this would be an enormous sum, perhaps half our national income, and would require a severe cut in private luxuries, but what a difference it would make to the nations of the world and to ourselves!

It is a fact that our nation is so rich that it was able to spend some fifty billions of dollars a year on a war without appreciably lessening the standard of living of our land, that six millions are now unemployed and automation continues to shorten working hours as well as workers, that farmers are paid not to cultivate their lands while incredible amounts of surplus rot in storehouses—all this while two-thirds of the world's population goes without a proper meal and millions are in immediate danger of starvation.

If we are indeed our brother's keeper, all children of one Father in heaven, then what incredible feats could be achieved by this nation, if it only possessed the will to share its wealth with the poor of the world! The Hebrew word for charity, *tzedakah,* does not mean charity at all. For "charity" has the overtones of doing something you do not have to do, going beyond what is required, being merciful and compassionate, deserving gratitude. *Tzedakah* means nothing of the sort. It means quite literally, "doing what is right." It is right that the rich share with the poor, because the wealth of the rich man does not belong to him. "The earth is the Lord's and the fullness thereof," wrote the Psalmist, echoing the meaning of the Sabbatical and Jubilee laws of return of property to their original owners, which established the teaching of Biblical economics—justice! To take our economics quite literally from the Bibilcal source, which in fact as a Christian country we claim to uphold, would be one of the most revolutionary acts in the history of mankind. It would mean circumscribing the pleasures and luxuries of a prosperous, lazy, soft America; doing without new autos, electrical gadgets, stylish clothes and being restricted to *necessities;* utilizing our manpower and our entire production power, not for ourselves alone, but for the newly emerging nations of the world, as well as for the over-populated areas of the earth where terror threatens—and incidentally providing our own country with the schools, the cleanliness, the welfare, the public needs, that is befitting the wealthiest nation on earth; doing *without* things because others need them; *giving* to others because we own nothing.

All this sounds like some utopian fantasy of the nineteenth century. In actuality it is the sanest economic policy we could follow. It should be accepted, of course, not for its utilitarian wisdom, but for the sake of the justice which informs it, and which ever demanded from man and nation responsible stewardship. Yet today it appears to be the essence of practical wisdom. Once again the Bible calls out to us across the centuries, the most practical of books—and its message—a matter of life and death.

World Law

Biblical faith is universal; it is not located within particular nations; its message is for all mankind. True, history has divided us into tongues, peoples, and even Biblical faith has fragmented. But the vision is the same.

> And it shall come to pass in the end of days,
> That the mountain of the Lord's house shall be established
> As the top of the mountains,
> And shall be exalted above the hills;
> And all nations shall flow into it.
> And many peoples shall go and say:
> "Come ye, and let us go up to the mountain of the Lord,
> To the house of the God of Jacob;
> And he will teach us of His ways,
> And we will walk in His paths."
> For out of Zion shall go forth the law,
> And the word of the Lord from Jerusalem
> And He shall judge between the nations,
> And shall decide for many peoples;
> And they shall beat their swords into plowshares,
> And their spears into pruning-hooks;
> Nation shall not lift up sword against nation,
> Neither shall they learn war any more.

The longing to repair the breach within mankind—"Have we not all one Father? Has not one God created us?"—which has lain dormant in the heart of the Biblical faiths, has ceased to be merely a utopian vision and has become what it was always meant to be, a matter of life and death. It is difficult to comprehend how people can prefer the risks of atomic war to those of world government, except that they suffer from an illusion fostered over the centuries that nations are inviolate, that to protect national interests the use of power is justified, that wars provide glory, that any military destruction can be repaired within a single generation, that one must beware of internationalists, and that America must in the end destroy Russia.

But we are now in the atomic age—Arnold Toynbee told the international assemblage convened to discuss Pope John's *Pacem in Terris*—and so we cannot survive if we continue . . . the old senseless and barbarous method of resorting to force. The accelerating pace of technological advance is making it increasingly difficult to solve our problems on any scale short of a world-wide one. We have to make war impossible, we have to save the human race from being poisoned by the waste product of "atoms for peace" and we are soon going to have to feed three or four times as many people as are now alive. I believe these jobs can be dealt with only by world authorities with effective power to override the national governments. The mutual interest of all nations is that the human race shall survive. If the nations destroy the human race, they will be destroying themselves with it. Therefore it is the mutual interest of the nations to subordinate their national sovereignty to world authorities. This is the only condition on which the nations can survive in the atomic age.

It is the task of the Biblical faiths, as well as those of the Far East, to shatter the present illusions and quicken the ancient vision by preaching the obsolescence of sovereign nations in a world which is joined by the threat of death, and by teaching the spiritual oneness of man under the oneness of God as the only enduring ground for political unity.

World Opinion

The Biblical faiths can stretch out their arms in brotherhood to all other religions. The impending destruction of mankind should be the ever-present issue before the world's religions, mobilizing their strength in a global effort to preserve man. A world congress of religion dedicated to the survival of human life could be a step in awakening the conscience of the nations to its common danger. How is it possible not to forget theological distinctions, philosophic quarrels, and historical schisms in order to bring the spiritual forces of all humanity together in such an undertaking? Jew, Protestant, Catholic, Moslem, Hindu, whatever their differences, passionately agree upon one thing: the necessity of halting mankind's reckless road to ruin. Indeed, it appears so unreal that some such total religious effort has not already been begun, as to question whether the world religions, enmeshed in their peculiar theological and political problems, truly comprehend, what God wants from man.

The ecumenical movement progresses among the many Protestant denominations, the Greek Orthodox, and the Catholic church; Judaism, Islam, and the far-Eastern religions are all subjects from time to time of polite and even serious mutual inquiry—"conversations" as they are called—but what has happened to the inner core of these great faiths? Should not the rumblings of the approaching catastrophe shatter the measure of their ordinary and even extraordinary agendas and cause them to move in unprecedented action to a true joining of hands across oceans, continents, colors, and faiths, not because of any desire to merge churches, but because we are indeed *already* merged in this venture against the common enemy? All religion is ultimately an attempt to relate man to the mystery of the universe. Can anything be of more concern to all religion than the possible end of that divine experiment called man? For if that happens, salvation, prayer, mercy, and sacrament will have no meaning whatsoever.

Men throughout the world stand in dread of the future and wait for a clarion call to action which can halt the seemingly inevitable. The day after Kruschev cynically announced a resumption of nuclear testing, promising a one hundred megaton "doomsday" bomb, thus rendering all the months of meetings in Geneva to arrive at a permanent ban as nothing but delaying tactics, some of the so-called "neutral" nations meeting in Belgrade cried treachery, deceit, horror—and the following letter by a distinguished scientist appeared in the *New York Times* of September 2, 1961:

> Owing to the testing decision of the Soviet Union, the United States can now score a major political advance by dramatic action and by our refusal to follow the U. S. S. R.

Political gains that are now feasible far outweigh gains from adding to United States nuclear overkill capacity. There is world-wide fear of the arms race. Even the Soviet Government has been divided on the issue of testing.

Let us organize a world-wide pressure on the Soviets to desist from this deadly move. Let us appeal formally to all Governments and informally to all populations, especially the Soviet, to stop the renewed arms race. Let us call for a protest by silent assembly in every Soviet city at the same time and place. Let us inform the Soviet people and every developing country that the costly arms race shatters hope for better food, clothing and housing.

Let us declare our plans and our will for controlled disarmament. Let us call on the United Nations General Assembly to consider them.

Let us act as the conscience of mankind rather than as automatic followers of deadly move.

Do we doubt the effectiveness of such tactics? Are are aware of the universal undercurrent of horror at the approaching holocaust which is currently running through the minds of men in every nation, even those where the truth is not proclaimed and who might be reached? What could the collective voice of religion, the "conscience" of man, achieve if directed toward such a goal? Imagine the wave of revulsion rising in land after land, the determination following that revulsion, and the effects such determination might have upon political leaders, even beyond their borders!

Religious leaders could create an international body whose task it would be to awaken the human race to the terror which lies ahead and to urge, on a spiritual basis, that change of heart and mind which might provide a lasting basis to a nuclear test ban agreement, disarmament, renunciation of national sovereignty, and that new world which must arise out of the present crisis, if we are to survive! It is not for such a congress to formulate a complete program, but rather to direct each to work in his own way, through the tradition, symbols, and sacraments of his own respective faith, for those general goals which can be agreed upon by all. America, for example, is not aware of the real crisis ahead; it prefers to move nonchalantly along the path of pleasure and business as usual: even the United States Congress reflects no genuine alertness at times. Consider what the united forces of American religion could do from weekly pulpit, classes, and publications to bring about that sense of national purpose, personal sacrifice, and inner transformation which must be achieved to face the almost impossible demands of the present and the rapidly darkening future. And, if some such action is not determined upon in the near future, there is reason to fear that a growing number of religious groups may be drawn into the deepening, despondent pacifist position.

Christianity arose in part because it believed that the redeemer had come, that history was at an end. What infinite strength then emerged from the untouched depths of the human heart, what miracles were wrought by ordinary men, what number of lives were transformed from self-seeking to self-sacrifice. A way of purity and devotion was fashioned so strongly that a new society grew up around it, established with power so enormous that it lives on even when history did not end but continued. If this could happen to a small band of men because of the *belief* which they held, imagine what could happen today if we allowed the *knowledge*—not belief—that the world might indeed come to an end to enter human consciousness through the channels of radical religion! Powers undreamt of would rise from the untouched chambers of the human soul, so genuine, so momentous, so total, as to wither the old self in a moment of contrition, direct the new self to the goal now conceived, and furnish unending waters from the well of the spirit to govern, decide, and act.

What is proposed for world spirit could be paralleled by world intellect. The universities of the world could meet in an international gathering for the same purpose: to consider that threat to annul or to so malform and decimate human life that the further existence of mankind would be in question. Universities everywhere are devoted to the accumulation and dissemination of knowledge, but if the moment arrives when *homo sapiens,* for whom this knowledge is acquired, is himself in danger of extinction, would it not seem obvious that unprecedented means must be sought by that part of society to treat the problem, not when and if the spirit moves them individually, but as the result of world-wide congresses whose purpose it would be to establish the problem of human survival as the central problem of all university concern, everywhere? In this fashion a good portion of the intellectual machinery of the entire world might be focused on this problem; the students of the world would be quick to comprehend and act, providing inestimable power in every local and national community to the solution of this most pressing problem of man.

I find it incredible that (1) men of spiritual concern do not see the one problem which now encompasses all others, and respond with at least the power they would if, for example, a thousand houses of worship of all faiths, were simultaneously blown up, and that (2) men of intellectual acumen who employ the deductive method in a far-reaching manner do not deduce from the available facts the conclusion which moves closer and closer to the line of inevitability and respond with at least the power they would if, for example, all text books throughout the world were on one day burned in vast pyres. Great is the need for the mobilization as a single unit of two of the vastest, most influential, and genuinely significant forces in the world today to deal with the problem of human survival.

CONCLUSION

The hand of the Lord was upon Me,
And he carried me out in the spirit of the Lord,
And set me down in the midst of the valley;
And it was full of bones;
And he caused me to pass by them round about;
And behold, there were very many in the open valley;
And lo, they were very dry.
And he said unto me, Son of man, can these bones live?
And I answered, O lord God, thou knowest.
Again he said unto me, Prophesy over these bones,
And say unto them, O ye dry bones, hear the word of
the Lord.
Thus saith the Lord God unto these bones: Behold,
I will cause breath to enter into you, and ye shall live.
And I will lay sinews upon you,
And will bring up flesh upon you,
And cover you with skin,
And put breath in you,
And ye shall live;
And ye shall know that I am the Lord.
So I prophesied as I was commanded;
And as I prophesied, there was a noise,
And behold an earthquake,
And the bones came together, bone to his bone.
And I beheld, and lo, there were sinews upon them,
And flesh came up, and skin covered them above:
But there was no breath in them.
Then said he unto me,
Prophesy unto the wind, prophesy, son of man, and say
to the wind,
Thus saith the Lord God: Come from the four winds, O
breath,
And breathe upon these slain, that they may live.
So I prophesied as he commanded me,
And the breath came into them,
And they lived, and stood up upon their feet,
An exceeding great army.
Then he said unto me,
Son of man, these bones are the whole house of Israel:
Behold, they say,

Our bones are dried up, and our hope is lost; we are
clean cut off.
Therefore prophesy, and say unto them,
Thus saith the Lord God: Behold, I will open your graves,
And cause you to come up out of your graves, O my
people;
And I will bring you into the land of Israel.
And ye shall know that I am the Lord,
When I have opened your graves,
And caused you to come up out of your graves,
O my people.
And I will put my spirit in you, and ye shall live.

                                                   (*Ezekiel* 11:13-18)

10

Conclusion

L<small>ET ME REVIEW</small> the substance of the argument I have attempted to present by referring to the concluding pages of Karl Jaspers' notable essay.

Inasmuch as mankind refuses to perish, the states will have to accept restrictions on their sovereign powers. What took place within limited areas when the original states were founded, must take place again; a voluntary association of states must be formed. The possibility of extreme disaster, which superior intelligence has brought about, is to be eliminated by a technique of institutional arrangements for the effective enforcement of treaties. If this could be done, mankind would not have to change. Intelligently devised institutions would, by the common will of all prevent any individual from making malevolent use of man's fundamental impulses—his drive to violent acts, his pleasure in violence and recklessness, his drive to go on and on to ever greater adventures, to escape the shallowness of actual existence. Under collective rule these impulses would have to be gratified in ways that do not imperil the whole of mankind.

But all of this has not been achieved so far. Political considerations tending toward such a goal are certainly the right ones. We must never give up trying to follow that path—the only practicable one; here planning is possible, and perhaps we can make some headway. But it is not enough. We have to ask whether treaties and institutions suffice to get rid of evil. May they not, rather develop into sham entities, behind which each state will simply go on strengthening its own power positions, preparing for the worst? In the meantime, tremendous resources and the best minds available today are being used to increase the numbers and the effectiveness of atom bombs, to make total death more possible. The eventuality draws closer day by day and year by year. It was the Second World War that enabled this to come to pass. Such enormous sums of money would not otherwise have been spent on anything so problematical of accomplishment, so totally unprofitable over a long stretch of time; in America it was fear of Hitler that set the thing in motion. What keeps it going is that war is still possible. It will stop only when war itself becomes impossible—war, which has existed as long as mankind, and the end of which seems impossible precisely because human nature is what it is. . . .

Malice and stupidity, hitherto limited in their consequences, are today dragging all mankind to its destruction. Unless we henceforward live all for one and each for all, we shall perish together. This unprecedented situation requires a response to scale. The response was given long ago. It looks beyond politics, and it has often been repeated since the prophets of the Old Testament first daringly uttered it and passed it on to all future ages. Because it has so often been repeated in vain, sometimes seriously and sometimes unseriously over the centuries, many have become weary of it. Now, however, we must face the extraordinary challenge of an extraordinary situation urgently imposed: we must transform our outlook and our ways of thinking, our moral-political will. An idea that has long been present in individuals, but has so far remained powerless, has become the condition of the survival of mankind. I believe I am not exaggerating. Those who go on living just as they lived before have not grasped the danger. Merely to conceive it intellectualy does not mean that it has been absorbed into the reality of one's life. Without a change of heart the life of mankind is lost forever. To survive, man must change. If he thinks only of the moment, everything will come to an end, almost certainly the day the atom war breaks out.

The change can only be brought about by each and every man in his own conduct of life: first within himself, and then in the realization that he is not alone. Every tiniest deed, every smallest word, every nuance of behavior among the millions and billions who are alive, is important. What takes place on the large and public scale is merely a symptom of that which is done in private by the many. . . . The statesman who makes a highly moral appeal at the conference table and then behaves disloyally at home, shares in the responsibility for the continuation of the evil he warns against. . . . If in his official capacity he displays tolerance for the human and all-too-human, while careless in the conduct of his own life, he undermines the spirit of the whole upon which we all count. The man who strives to bring about the miracle of a moral transformation in all mankind and yet contributes with his whole intelligence to the essentially thoughtless continuation of the existing state of affairs—perhaps by recourse to statements that have become empty the better to veil the truth—that man casts suspicion on morality itself.

When everything that can be protected in thought moves into the political arena, something will surely happen that cannot be foreseen. At this point the question, what are we to do? can no longer be answered by directions as to how it is to be done: the question can only be answered by an appeal to slumbering possibilities. Conversion is not enforceable. All we can do is to point to realities and make articulate the voices that for centuries have been calling for a change of heart. All that men can know of the possibilities of the future should

*be incorporated in the curricula of our schools. Whether
the individual will be affected thereby is a matter we
must leave to the freedom of the young. Once the fundamental facts of our political existence today are made
clear, and the consequences of the various modes of possible behavior have been developed, the answer is up to
each individual, not as a matter of opinion, but in the
full context of his life.*

*Total destruction was often mentioned by the ancient
prophets. The "Day of Yahweh" will come when everything will be destroyed. The early Christians spoke of an
impending end of the world. Today, such perspectives
have once again become unavoidable, this time in consequence of technological developments. Except for those
who live thoughtlessly from day to day, they must once
again become the central preoccupation of our life. Even
though we cannot safely rely on reason in men, is there
nonetheless some basis left for confidence? When despair
says: Nothing avails—let us not think about it—let us
live for the present—what lies in store for us is death in
any case—is this really the last word, is there really
nothing left after that? No, was Jeremiah's reply to his
despairing disciple Baruch, when the state and the nation
and even the religion of the Jews, become worshipers of
Isis, lay in ruins: "The Lord saith thus: Behold, that
which I have built will I break down, and that which I
have planted I will pluck up . . . And seekest thou great
things for thyself? Seek them not: For, behold, I will
bring evil upon all flesh." What Jeremiah meant was:
that God is enough.*

*This, and this only, is the ultimate horizon, in the
perspective of which everything falls into its right place.
It is here that courage grows out of confidence in the
ultimate ground of Being, which no worldly shipwreck
can destroy, not even the shipwreck of reason. Then
wings are given to the will, our will to achieve, to venture,
to see purpose in the process of building within human
existence so long as human existence lasts, even if we
do not know how long our achievements will endure.*

What Jaspers has written, almost as a last will and testament to his generation, and what I have endeavored to examine and clarify, is no mystical spiritualism which redeems man by removing his soul from his body, his self from his world. It is no attempt to separate man from his society, nor was that the message of the prophets. It is rather to transform society by looking at the world through a new dimension, the holy dimension. No longer is it man and the world, but man, God, and the world—man, God's word, and the world. Between man and his world stands that power, peace and plenty, which is the will of God and the presence of God. It is this sense of God's will and God's presence that modern man has lost, sundering himself from the very roots of his existence. The ultimate must once again become real so that it possesses the strength to transform, interpenetrating the disciplines of our society with new power and new perspective.

To revere God and walk in His way is, of course, no easy solution. I am not saying that it is, holding a simple formula aloft as the magic removal from all our ills. Far from it. Neither did Jaspers lay down any blueprint for the new society that may come. That is a project of gigantic proportions. I am only making one claim—that the material world is dependent, in the last analysis, upon the spiritual world, that ultimate realities have become immediate realities, and that our world may be annihilated unless we awake.

This is what we face, and these are its consequences.

The machinery for instant death for all mankind is now in man's hands.

There is no defense.

Only the creation of a new society can prevent the use of the bomb and outlaw war.

A new society requires a new man who can only become so by revering God and walking in His ways.

*   *   *

Sing, O barren, thou that didst not bear,
Break forth into singing, and cry aloud, thou that didst
    not travail;
For more are the children of the desolate
Than the children of the married wife, saith the Lord.

Enlarge the place of thy tent,
And let them stretch forth the curtains of thy habitations, spare not;
Lengthen thy cords, and strengthen thy stakes.
For thou shalt spread abroad on the right hand and on the left;
And thy seed shall possess the nations,
And make the desolate cities to be inhabited.
Fear not, for thou shalt not be ashamed.
Neither be thou confounded, for thou shalt not be put to shame;
For thou shalt forget the shame of thy youth,
And the reproach of thy widowhood shalt thou remember no more.
For thy Maker is thy husband,
The Lord of hosts is His name;
And the Holy One of Israel is thy Redeemer,
The God of the whole earth shall He be called.
For the Lord hath called thee
As a wife forsaken and grieved in spirit;
And a wife of youth, can she be rejected?
Saith thy God.
For a small moment have I forsaken thee;
But with great compassion will I gather thee.
In a little wrath I hid My face from thee for a moment;
But with everlasting kindness will I have compassion on thee,
Saith the Lord thy Redeemer.
For this is as the waters of Noah unto Me;
For as I have sworn that the waters of Noah
Should no more go over the earth,
So have I sworn that I would not be wroth with thee,
Nor rebuke thee.
For the mountains may depart,
And the hills be removed;
But my kindness shall not depart from thee,
Neither shall my covenant of peace be removed,
Saith the Lord that hath compassion on thee.

(Isaiah 54:1-10)

And it shall come to pass in latter days,
That the mountain of the Lord's house shall be established in the top of the mountains,
And it shall be exalted above the hills;
And peoples shall flow unto it.
And many nations shall go and say,
"Come ye, and let us go up to the mountain of the Lord,
And to the house of the God of Jacob;
And He will teach us of His ways, and we will walk in his paths."
For out of Zion shall go forth the law,
And the word of the Lord from Jerusalem.
And He shall judge between many peoples,
And shall reprove strong nations afar off;
And they shall beat their swords into plowshares, and their spears into pruning hooks:
Nation shall not lift up sword against nation,
Neither shall they learn war any more.
But they shall sit every man under his vine and under his fig tree;
And none shall make them afraid:
For the mouth of the Lord of hosts hath spoken it.

(*Micah* 4:1-4)

The Lord our God be with us, as He was with our fathers:
Let Him not leave us, nor forsake us:
That He may incline our hearts unto Him, to walk in all His ways,
And to keep His commandments, and His statutes, and His judgments,
Which He commanded our fathers.

(*I Kings* 8:57-58)

The eternal God is thy dwelling place,
And underneath are the everlasting arms.

(*Deut.* 32:27)

POSTSCRIPT

THE ARGUMENT of this book is clear: the radical nature of the nuclear threat is such that military and defense means alone cannot prevent atomic war, only a change in man himself. But can man change? Have we lost hope in man? Deep at the root of the unrest which pervades our time, manifesting itself in rising juvenile crimes, family breakdown, the collapse of sex mores, political cynicism and a fun morality, is the growing sense of human helplessness, as though we were drifting inexorably toward oblivion and carrying with us, bit by bit, the landmarks of culture and civilization.

How precious, then, those who demonstrate faith in the power of man. Among those who do is Moral Rearmament.

After concluding this manuscript, I by chance attended a conference sponsored by Moral Rearmament at Mackinac Island, Michigan. It brought me into contact with a world movement which sheds light on and breathes hope into the dire pages that have preceded. Some one thousand college students and three hundred men and women were gathered from all parts of America—Negro, Indian and white—as well as some from Europe, South America and Japan. They had come to learn how they could play a role in remaking the world. Most, I am sure, were at first filled with the same sense of despair which dominates our time and has done so much to undercut the yearnings of the younger generation.

At Mackinac they were given a new sense of purpose, a belief that America can be changed, that they can play a part in changing it, and that if it is to be changed, they must begin with themselves. The formula was simple: the ultimate problem is a moral problem. We treat it by treating ourselves first. We begin by setting right what is wrong with ourselves, then we can go on to the problems of society around us—the problems of political corruption, of labor and management, of Communism and even of atomic war.

What is so refreshing about Moral Rearmament, despite its apparent naivete, is that it tries to go to the heart of things, to the soul of the individual man. And achieving a breakthrough there, taps unmeasured quantities of spiritual energy for action around us, energy we never knew we had because we had not turned it in this direction and which startles us when we begin to feel it.

If the essence of the dilemma is that without a change in man our world cannot be saved, then Moral Rearmament, utilizing the insights of prophetic religion, makes a significant contribution in helping us understand that human nature can indeed be transformed by providing an individual discipline of moral purification, an exemplary brotherhood of workers and a program of action which demonstrates from time to time how in concrete situations, often thought to be purely diplomatic, political or economic, concern for the moral dimension may be decisive in moving toward a solution.

ACKNOWLEDGMENT

THE AUTHOR would like to express his appreciation to the following for permission to reprint excerpts from their publications.

John Bennett; Bernard Brodie, *Strategy in the Missile Age,* Princeton University Press, Princeton, N. J. 1959, 1963; Harrison Brown and James Real, *Community of Fear,* the Fund for the Republic Inc., Santa Barbara, California; Martin Buber; Vivian Cadden, *Children and the Bomb,* Redbook, Nov. 1962; Rachel Carson, *Silent Spring,* Houghton Mifflin Co., Boston, 1962; Whittaker Chambers, *Cold Friday,* Random House, N. Y. 1964; Whittaker Chambers, *Witness,* Random House, N. Y. 1952; Comer Clarke, *Eichmann, the Man and his Crimes,* Ballantine Books, N. Y. 1960; editorial, Jan. 2, 1909, *Christian Century;* Norman Corwin, *Overkill and Megalove,* World Publishing Co., N. Y.; Dr. Louis Finkelstein, *The United Synagogue Review;* Dr. Jerome Frank; Frank Gibney, *The Operators,* Harper, N. Y. 1960; Abraham Heschel, *Between God and Man,* Harper, N. Y.; Abraham Heschel, *The Earth is the Lord's,* Abelard-Schuman, N. Y. 1950; Keneth Heuer, *The Next Fifty Billion Years,* Viking, N. Y. 1957; Rolf Hochhuth, *The Deputy,* Grove Press Inc., N. Y. 1964; William Hull, *The Struggle for a Soul,* Doubleday, New York 1963; Karl Jaspers, *The Atom Bomb and the Future of Man,* Grove Press Inc., N. Y.; Editorial, *Life Magazine,* Aug. 15, 1961; Walter Lippman; Walter Miller, *A Canticle for Leibowitz,* J. B. Lippincott, N. Y.; Muste; Arch Obler, *The Night of the Auk,* Horizon Press Publishers, N. Y.; *The Scandal of Our Missile Program,* by Kenneth O. Gilmore, Readers Digest, August 1961; Sabatier; Max Scheler, *The Eternal in Man,* Harper, N. Y., 1960; Sir Charles Snow; John Steinbeck; Stillman and Pfaff, *The New Politics,* Coward-McCann, New York, 1961; Tom Stonier, *Nuclear Disaster,* Meridian Books, N. Y. 1963; *Roads that Bypass Peace,* Norman Thomas, the Saturday Review; *Theology and Modern Warfare,* J. C. Murray in *Morality in Modern Warfare,* ed. by W. Nagle, Helicon Press, Baltimore 1960. Samuel Dresner, *The Jew in American Life,* Crown Publishers, N. Y., 1963.

Special thanks is due to Mrs. Elliot Potter for her kindly assistance in the preparation of this book.

IF YOU ENJOY LIVING

YOU WILL LIVE WITH

LIVING BOOKS:

THE RABBI WHO NEVER DIED

By Samuel H. Dresner

IN THE MIRROR OF LITERATURE

By William M. Glicksman

EMANCIPATION AND ADJUSTMENT

By David Rudavsky

PANORAMA OF JUDAISM   *By Leo Jung*

TIMES SQUARE—CROSSROAD OF THE WORLD
CHINATOWN — NEW YORK
TEENS ON A TIGHTROPE
ISLES OF THE DEVIL
IN THIS LIFE AND THE NEXT
THE HERMIT OF S'DE BOKER
LEGENDS AND TALES FROM EVERYWHERE

By Philip Paneth

CRISIS IN T.V.   *By Solomon Simonson*

AFRICAN ODYSSEY   *By John L. Brom*

THE POLITICAL PLATYPUS   *By Emery Kelen*

BUDDHA IS MY REFUGE   *By Boris Erwitt*

SPIES AND SPYING   *By Ladislas Farago*

THE FOUNDING FATHERS OF THE BIBLE

By Abraham I. Katch

MY OCCULT DIARY   *By Cornelius Tabori*

THE ANGEL COMETH   *By Leonard S. Friedman*

THE CRISIS OF MARRIAGE   *By Philippe d'Alba-Julien*

VOYAGE TO FAREMIDO * CAPILLARIA

By Frigyes Karinthy

A COMMUNITY IN STRESS   *By Whitney H. Gordon*

YOUR CHANGING WORLD   *By Philip Shorr*

IF CHRIST CAME TO CHICAGO

By William T. Stead

IF CHRIST CAME TO CONGRESS

By Milford W. Howard